Wakefield Press

NO PLACE LIKE HOME

Sonja Dechian is a scriptwriter for ABC Asia Pacific. She has a Masters in creative writing and her short fiction has been published in a range of books and journals.

Jenni Devereaux is a researcher and writer with the Australian Education Union. She is active in Australians Against Racism projects and in campaigns for human and labour rights.

Heather Millar is a freelance writer and editor who has worked on a range of magazines and books in Australia and England.

Eva Sallis is a writer of literary fiction. Her most recent novels are *The Marsh Birds*, *Fire Fire* and *Mahjar*.

NO PLACE LIKE HOME

AUSTRALIAN STORIES
by young writers aged 8–21 years

Edited by Sonja Dechian, Jenni Devereaux,
Heather Millar and Eva Sallis

Wakefield
Press

Wakefield Press
16 Rose Street
Mile End
South Australia 5031
wakefieldpress.com.au

First published 2005

Cover painting by Abbas Mehran
Cover designed by Liz Nicholson, designBITE
Text designed by Clinton Ellicott, Wakefield Press
Typeset by Michael Deves

National Library of Australia Cataloguing-in-publication entry

No place like home: Australian stories.
ISBN 978 1 86254 686 8.
1. Short stories, Australian – 21st century. 2. Children's writings, Australian.
3. Youths' writings, Australian. I. Dechian, Sonja.

A823.01089283

CORIOLE
McLAREN VALE

Wakefield Press thanks
Coriole Vineyards for
continued support

CONTENTS

Something about Love

Foreword

by Eva Sallis

All these stories on the theme of home are of journeys: stories of homes lost and homes gained. Perhaps it is inevitable that a narrative picture of home in Australia is built through a mosaic of journey stories: we are all displaced peoples or the descendents of displaced peoples, whether we are from Indigenous, settler, migrant or refugee families. Perhaps we only fully understand what home means when we lose it, or have to remake it. Our journeys or the journeys of our recent ancestors were sometimes forced, sometimes voluntary. In all, exile and the making of a new home are themes that give us some of the most potent Australian stories.

These stories were collected through two nationwide writing competitions run in 2002 and 2004 by Australians Against Racism Inc, a creative grassroots human rights and social justice organisation that was formed in 2001. Both competitions asked young people to use an interview or a direct personal experience of displacement as their starting point, and then left them free to choose whether to write their story as fiction or essay. The quality of stories was exceptional. The striking thing in each year was how passionate, eloquent and effective young people are when they have something important to say, either from their discoveries in interview, or from their own experience. For many writers, this was an opportunity to make their voice heard on some of the burning issues of our times. For others, it was a chance to tell their own extraordinary stories, or the stories that form part of their family heritage.

Following the competition in 2002, we edited the hugely successful anthology *Dark Dreams: Australian Refugee Stories by Young Writers aged 11–20 Years*, published by Wakefield Press in early 2004. *No Place Like Home* is both the second anthology in what we hope will be a series, and unique. It is a development from that first experimental project, driven by the idea of recording not just the range of refugee stories that young people can encounter, but by having young people discover and reveal the essence of being Australian. The diversity of stories we received will be clear from this volume.

The stories presented in this anthology are a small sample of the stories we received. Selection was a hard and painful process, as many superb stories had to be left out. The stories you read here in most cases have been only lightly edited. We have preserved almost all idioms and choices in the voices of young writers using English as a second language: in many cases this pressured English is extraordinarily moving and dignified, and has an energy all its own.

This volume includes stories of hatred and tolerance; rejection and love; acceptance and alienation; war, aftermath and resolution; fear and hope; great suffering and great heroism; small journeys and unimaginably huge journeys. These young writers have something important to say to all Australians, young and old. For me these young voices share a theme beyond any notion of Australia as the homeland of many displaced people. These stories all suggest the preciousness and fragility of belonging and the importance and irreplaceable nature of each human life and experience.

Eva Sallis
President, Australians Against Racism Inc., 2005

MYSTERIOUS JOURNEYS

'This is my retelling of a great man who lost everything to a silly colour believing. It's up to the children of today to stop this, so please DON'T let it happen again.'

Felicity Rose Hann

Hal Hart's Story

by Felicity Rose Hann, aged 12

Hal and his sister Cheryl were coming out of the old school doors when a police officer of quite a big build offered them a ride home. Being a foolish young ten-year-old boy, Hal said, 'Oh yeah cool,' but his sister disagreed.

'Oh come on Cheryl, how often are we going to get a ride in a motor car?'

'I don't think we should. Think of what Mama would say.'

'Please,' Hal said, with his innocent look. Mama and Cheryl always caved in when he did that look.

'Oh all right, get in.'

'Yes! Thank you Cheryl. Mr Policeman, we would like to go for that ride please.'

'Good. Jump in,' said the police officer, opening the door.

'Hal, don't tell Mama,' Cheryl said with a stern look.

'I won't.'

That was the last time Hal ever saw the old school building. You see, Hal was one of the stolen generation. The stolen generation started in the 1900s and didn't stop until 1990. Pretty recent huh? The government took Aboriginal children away from their parents, put them in homes and tried to bring them up without their natural culture. Let me break it down for you. Say alien Martians came to earth and took you away and tried to teach you the way they live while breaking every single rule in your culture. Cruel isn't it?

Anyway just thought you might need some background information, so let's get back to the story.

'Cheryl, we missed the turn-off to our house twenty minutes ago. Where's he taking us?'

'I don't know, ask him.'

'Mister. We missed the turn-off to our house.'

'It's okay, I know, I just thought you might like to go for a bit of a drive. I'll take you home soon.'

But Hal and Cheryl were never taken home. They were taken to Darwin and separated, never to see each other again.

'Lights out, children, you've got an early start tomorrow. Good night.' Matron turned out the lights. Hal was confused. He didn't know where he was or where he was going. The dormitory was quiet except for the sobbing – there was always crying at night, you could never stop it. These children had the exact same problem as Hal. They were all children of the stolen generation. Hal was only one of one hundred thousand.

'Up children, you've got a big journey to Croker Island.' Croker Island. That name would be stuck in Hal's head for the rest of his life.

He got up and pulled on the clothes Matron had laid out for him at the end of his bed. The array included an ugly old green sweater that was dusty and smelt like dead fish, a pair of jeans that were much too big for him and a pair of shoes that were so old his toes stuck out the end. All the boys were told to go in one part of the courtyard while the girls were told to go in the other. From there the boys were separated if they had the same language. Hal was sent with twelve other boys. The boys all seemed to have their own characteristics. Hal tried to say hello but they laughed at him. Hal was confused; he didn't understand why they laughed. Then he tried saying hello in English and he had much better results.

'Don't you speak the ways of the cicada people?'

'No, does anyone speak the ways of the dingos?' said a tall boy.

'How about the platypus tribe?' said a short stocky boy.

'Remember they split us up so no one in the same tribe is together?'

'Oh yeah.'

'Where they're taking us?'

'. . . right, number ones, follow me.' And a bunch of boys followed the man. The boys kept talking until the number eleven was called.

'And you boys will be taken to Croker Island. Into the boys home of blah, blah, BLAH ha ha ha,' and he led them to a ferry. 'This is your ride to the rest of your life – enjoy it.'

And he opened the ferry door and they all got in.

A couple of hours later Hal and his group arrived. It wasn't much different from Darwin. They drove him along with the bunch of boys to a big shed type thing. They were shown to a big room with four beds. 'This is where you will be staying,' said their new matron.

'But, miss, there are only four beds. Where will the rest of us stay?' asked the short boy.

'Well, there are twelve of you and four beds, so three to a bed and four beds makes twelve.'

'Great,' Hal heard a plumpish sort of boy murmur.

That night Hal started thinking of ways he could escape. *What about if I call to the spirits and get the great eagle to save me?* He tried but nothing happened. *What if I build a boat? Grandad taught me how*, and he started building the boat in his head.

'If I do this . . . and that . . .' he murmured to himself. But he never managed it.

He awoke the next morning to a very noisy bell.

'Five minutes till prayer meeting.'

'Prayer meeting? What's a prayer meeting?' he said, puzzled.

'Well, put it this way – if you don't want a flogging, RUN!'

So he ran and ran until he found it. He was just in time, but one of the other boys was just two or three minutes after him.

'Everybody will witness this punishment so that none of you newies fall out of line,' said a very big man, and with that he picked up his whip and gave the boy such a flogging that Hal never forgot. He tried the best he could from that moment on to be a model student.

Three years passed. Then came the time when Hal and all his friends were to be taken somewhere else for their secondary schooling.

'Hal, which school would you like to go to?' said Freddy their man matron, holding a map of Australia.

'I would like to go here, sir,' he said, pointing to Darwin.

'But you cannot go there because it is too close to where you used to live.'

'Well what about this Adelideee?' said Hal, thinking about his old teacher from Darwin.

'You mean Adelaide,' said Freddy with a chuckle. 'Okay, pack your stuff. You will be sent there tomorrow morning.'

Hal was sent to Adelaide where he finished all his schooling. He later came to my little town where he became president of my footy club. From there he retired and now enjoys the freedom and simplicity of life. This is my retelling of a great man who lost everything to a silly colour believing. It's up to the children of today to stop this, so please DON'T let it happen again.

Salima's Story

by Salima Haidary, Hallie Kent and Ramona Strang, aged 15

My name is Salima Haidary and this is my story. I was born in Ghazni, in a small town of Kabul, Afghanistan, in December 1988. Until the age of about eight I lived a fairly normal life for a girl in Afghanistan – a usual day was cleaning, cooking and sewing. I did not go to school because the Taliban didn't allow girls to have an education. Occasionally I was allowed to spend time with my friend. She lived in the house joined to mine, but I could not go and see her unless my father walked with me, as young girls and women were not allowed out on the streets on their own. If the Taliban soldiers found a woman out on her own they would kill her and leave her body where friends would see it as a warning.

I rarely got to see my father, as he had to hide from the Taliban. He hid because he did not want to fight for them. One morning he went in his truck to Kabul to sell some firewood and he never came home. The Taliban caught him and some of his friends and said they had to become soldiers. My father and his friends escaped and ran away to Pakistan – we never heard from him again until we had been in Canberra for ten months. After he had escaped, my home was visited regularly by soldiers asking where he was.

Just after I turned seven, soldiers were starting to fill the streets in small groups. Eventually they were everywhere. They all had a uniform of olive green pants, a long brown coat and big black boots. They had empty faces and they all had long, black beards. They carried guns that had a sharp knife on one end and a hard block-like object on the other. They abused anyone who didn't do what they were told or who got in their way. This is why my six-year-old brother died when I was ten. He was hit in the head with the end of the soldier's gun, because the soldiers thought he was lying about where my father was. This made us feel angry and afraid that they might do the same to us. The loss of my brother filled me with doubt that our family would ever be safe.

Not long after that my other little brother died. He was only four years old. One day the soldiers came again looking for my father. When they questioned my mother she told them, 'We don't know where he is.' The soldiers began beating her viciously with their guns, yelling, 'You lie, you lie!' My mother was holding my brother and she dropped him on the ground when the soldiers began to hit her. My brother's nose began to bleed, and then the blood came out of his mouth as well. We could not stop the blood and then he died. The soldiers found this amusing and while laughing they told my younger sister with a gun to her head that she was next. It was so frightening. Then they got my father's picture, the only thing that could remind us of him, and burned it to ashes.

After that we tried to keep on living our lives as normally as we could in such conditions. The gunshots and screaming did not ever seem to stop and everybody was always afraid. The windows were boarded and the locks on our doors were useless. At night the soldiers often came to our house. They would take our blankets, saying, 'Why are you sleeping with a blanket,' leaving us cold, sleepless and sick all the time. It made me feel helpless that my mother was always sad and she didn't want to live anymore. It was like her life had drained out of her body.

In every home there was fear and people were always crying.

There was never any happiness. When the soldiers were near your door you had to be very quiet, you even had to breathe quietly. You could never trust any man in the street because he might be a soldier. It had been four years and we hadn't heard anything from our father. There were no telephones or mail – there was no way he could contact us and we didn't know that he had escaped to Pakistan. We thought he had been killed.

One day my grandfather had had enough and he tried to convince my mother to take us and leave the country, pushing his lifesavings into her hands. At first my mother did not take the money, saying, 'I can't leave you here with nothing.' He replied, 'I am old. I have lived my life. Look at your children! They are always afraid and they have their whole lives ahead of them. They shouldn't die here.' Then she said, 'But I am a woman. What will I do? Where do I go? No one will listen to me or help me!' Then he slapped her across the face and said, 'LEAVE!' and walked away. I was so angry with my grandfather because he hit my mother, but now I can see that he saved us.

After my mother had stopped crying she stood up and said, 'We are leaving.' But I still didn't feel any hope. I kept thinking my mother was crazy. What was she getting us into? We would never survive. And I asked her, 'Where are we going? We will never get away, maybe we should stay.' When I said this, my mother got very angry and said, 'NO! We have to try and escape. If we stay we will just die and we wouldn't have tried. It's easy for your brothers and father, they are already dead.' After my mother said this I thought to myself, 'So what if we are women, we are the same and we can survive.'

We went home and packed only what we needed – water and bread. We walked for a whole night and a day and we were exhausted. We met three other families: two of them were also missing husbands and all three, the same as us, were fleeing from our country. They had a truck. They said we could travel with them so we would not have to walk anymore. The two men were driving but the women and children were forced to hide behind a stack of potatoes and tea. If we were discovered then we would have all been shot and the men would have been used as soldiers. We arrived in Pakistan and we stayed for three days in a cheap and dirty hotel, keeping out of sight. On the fourth day a man approached us and said, 'If you give me four thousand American dollars then I will get you to another country that is safe for your children, but you have to be very careful that the police or security don't see you.'

On the fifth day he returned and we left. We travelled by truck for three or four days. Our food was so low that we could only feed the younger children. After what seemed like forever we arrived in a place called Karachi. We stayed there overnight and the next day we were on a plane going to Indonesia. After a two hour trip, we arrived. There we stayed eleven days in a house that was very small, with a smell that was so bad I couldn't breathe. We had to share two bedrooms between four families. On the eleventh night we caught a bus – we travelled for five hours then we boarded a boat with three hundred and sixty other people.

The boat was so crowded! We had been promised a boat that had a room for every family, toilets in every room, a swimming pool and a restaurant! But the boat we had was very dirty and it seemed it would break apart at any time. There were three levels and I was stuck on the bottom level next to the engine; it was so loud and it smelled so bad and I felt so sick. People vomited over me, in my face and all over me. When people died they just threw their bodies into the sea. While we were in the middle of the ocean the boat broke down.

Luckily there was a man who knew a bit about mechanics and he fixed the boat – after that he was very popular! After four nights and four days we arrived on Christmas Island, Australia. But even though we were in Australia there were soldiers pointing guns at us. Our boat was told to go back by the police.

Although I was afraid of the guns I knew the soldiers were not like the soldiers back home. They put us in what looked like a big gym where we had lots and lots of food. I have never eaten so much in my life! Even when I wasn't hungry anymore I still kept eating. There were clean showers and toilets and everyone was always fighting, pulling hair, kicking and punching just to use the toilets. Even with all the fights, I thought, 'I have made it, we have survived!' After that we were sent to the detention centre in Port Hedland. We stayed there for three months, and, although it was safe, it was a lot like jail. We had very small rooms and the security guards were constantly checking on us, but I knew I wouldn't have to be afraid for my life.

After that we were sent to Canberra. I was so excited. I still can remember coming to Canberra at twelve o'clock at night and seeing all the lights of the city and thinking, *perhaps I am in heaven!* When I saw Parliament House, I thought it was made out of paper or something. Then we arrived at a hotel in Civic. It was like a palace, when I saw it I felt like a queen! It was so clean and we were not cramped anymore. When I saw the elevator I thought, *what is that?* When I got in and it started to go down, I was screaming and crying, then when it got to the kitchen, I was thinking, *it can read minds, WOW!* because it stopped when I reached the kitchen.

We stayed in a hotel for a couple of months, then finally moved to a house for people whose families have separated. We lived there for about ten months. One day when we came back from a picnic there was a phone call. I picked up the phone and a woman told me that there was a man in Canberra and maybe he was my father, but she told me not to tell the others because if it wasn't my father they would be so disappointed. The next day they arranged a meeting for my family and yes! It was our father and we were so happy because we had finally found him after five years. Now we were crying tears of joy!

After we found our father we had enough money to rent a

house for our family. My first day at school was very confusing. I didn't think I would make any friends but some people were nice to me and they stuck up for me when some students called me Osama Bin Laden's daughter. I was very shocked when they called me that. Also on the first day of school a lot of boys – there were about eleven or twelve of them – were trying to hit us with fruit. So we retaliated and pelted them with fruit. Soon I befriended three girls: Hallie, Ramona and Anne. They are good friends: they are always here for me when I need them and accept me for who I am. At the end of the year I met my teacher. My first impression of her was that she was okay, but I got to know her when school went back after the holidays – she was really nice so I told her my story. Now whenever I feel I need to talk to someone about something, I tell her because I know I can trust her.

Still we are waiting to see if we have to go back to Afghanistan. Always we are waiting and not knowing if we will stay or if we will go. It is very hard to live not knowing what will happen in your life. I thought I will kill myself if I have to go back. I'm afraid we will all be killed if we have to go back – the soldiers will punish us. My sister Fatima is five years old – all the time she asks me, 'How will the soldiers kill us when we go back?' and she cries every night. When I try to go to sleep every night I don't want to close my eyes because I see all the faces of dead people in the water.

If I stay in Australia I want to be a doctor or a nurse. If I was a doctor or a nurse I could have saved my little brother from bleeding to death.

But my story is better than the stories of others. At least I have some good times and I have learned how to laugh and be happy. I go to school and I have most of my family.

My name is Salima Haidary and this is my story.

Injustice – When You Can't Tell: Linda's Story

by Irene Guo, aged 12

I should be happy, excited, celebrating that the exam-free days are finally coming true. It is ten days until I graduate from high school. But there is so much gloom, dread and misery in the air that I could almost swim in it. Everyone is trying not to think of the future.

The government calls it The Great Proletarian Cultural Revolution. It's supposedly to 'get rid of unorthodox ideas and men suspected of holding them.'

Due to this revolution, senior leaders have been purged or demoted. University presidents and party secretaries were also purged or dropped. This made way for students of peasant backgrounds to be enrolled in these universities. Plus the government has already put the intellectuals, who are said to have 'unorthodox ideas', into prison.

Since all the places at universities are taken up with people with peasant backgrounds, this meant we, as the 'bourgeois' people, don't have a chance of going to universities after we finish high school. So instead of going to university, we are going to be transported out to the country to do agriculture. The government says it's to 'experience the hardships of the farmer', plus they say we have been studying so long we should know what labour feels like and we're to work there the rest of our lives. Anyone disagreeing is imprisoned for life.

These are all parts of The Great Proletarian Cultural Revolution. Everyone knows the government is just making an excuse to get the educated people of the younger generation out of the city so that they can seal our mouths shut so we can't tell everyone about the injustices of the government. This way we can't join forces to rebel against them. We are helpless and we can't voice our thoughts or we would be classified as men with unorthodox ideas and be shot or imprisoned.

The government is tearing our lives apart; they are taking away our parents, family and friends, the city we love and everything that we live for. They're doing this for themselves so they can secure their ruling powers. This is just barbaric and inhumane. We might be alive yet our spirit is dead.

The day I have been dreading so long has arrived. I'm hugging and kissing my parents, family and friends. Saying goodbye forever. I'll never see them again. Mum gives me a rib-breaking hug. I never want to let her go. I can feel the pain eating my insides, bursting my veins and setting my bones on fire. Yet the tears won't come.

I wave to my family all the way until they are out of sight. I feel as though someone has ripped out my heart and left me to bleed to death. It is pain beyond what I have experienced before. A wound that will never heal. Pain beyond what these words can ever tell.

I can hear people sobbing around me as we bump along the dry, dusty road.

Sweat drips down my forehead, the sun blazes overhead, burning the back of my neck. My back is aching from being bent all day; my arms are about to fall off from the endless digging. I can feel my stomach contract with hunger pains. I've been working from dawn to dusk and I get paid ¥1.10 a day. With this money I can only have one meal a day.

A month has gone by. I'm so tired and hungry I can barely stand up. Some people suggest we should escape and seek refuge in Hong Kong. We all know that Hong Kong is somewhere near the border of Guangdong. To get there we only have to swim about three kilometres. We've been looking at the border every day as we work in the rice fields. I can't believe I never thought of going to Hong Kong.

I really have no idea how we will survive in Hong Kong, but I know there is more chance of survival in Hong Kong than staying here and starving for the rest of my life. Not many want to come. They think our idea is crazy. But nothing is stopping me getting out of this place.

I cannot believe I am doing this. I lie awake on my bed, looking at my watch, waiting for it to strike midnight. 8:00, 9:00, 10:00, 11:00, 11:15, 11:30, 11:40, 11:50, 11:55. 11:59. 12:00!!! I tiptoe out of my bed. I see four shadows doing the same thing.

We crept out of the dormitory out into the rice fields and over the barbed wires. We were lucky that it was a cloudless night. I felt more secure with the silvery moon gliding along with us like a ghost. I felt I had nature's support.

The dry rocks along the sandy shores were crunching under my feet. The waves crashed onto the jagged rocks. I was one step closer to leaving hell. The only thing in my way was a body of water. It would be a tough swim.

We all took a deep breath in and a last look at our country. 'One, two, three . . . Go!'

SPLASH!!

Water gushed into my mouth and nose. I kicked my feet as fast as I could, I pushed my hands harder and harder. I wanted to get out of the sea quick and fast. I didn't know when the tide would set in. I didn't want to push my luck . . . Then . . .

SPOOSH!!!!

A huge wave crashed overhead. Water gushed into my mouth and up my nose. I could feel the salt water stinging my eyes. I felt the blood pound in my skull. My head was spinning. My chest was aching. I needed AIR!! I knew no more . . .

I close my eyes. It has been nearly a year since that wave that I thought was going to kill me washed me onto the shores of Hong Kong, yet I remember it like yesterday. I have been given Hong Kong citizenship. It is like heaven here compared to China. I can't believe that just over a body of water is the difference between heaven and hell.

This is my story, one of millions of stories out there. Many don't even live to tell the tale. Treasure your life. Never give up, because there are many people out there struggling to live on in hell.

Long Road to Happiness

by Jasmina Kevric, aged 18

She marks her presence in the wet sand, the waves surging around the indentations. The footprints follow her in the same way that her experiences will throughout her life. She stops and looks back. The footsteps seem to have a beginning but not an ending. The beauty of the sunset catches her eye. How lovely it feels to witness such an extraordinary event. How lovely it feels to be alive. She closes her eyes, tears rushing down her cheeks.

Her memories abruptly shift to a world filled with hate and terror. To a day she wishes never existed. To a time when the fight for survival was as tough as creating world peace. Standing in the middle of her backyard, she watched her grandparents and uncles returning from the farm. Her mother was inside baking bread while her younger brother was on his way towards the enormous plum tree a few metres in front of him. Noticing that she still had cherries in her hands, she called her brother to share them. He ran happily towards her. He opened his mouth and she threw a cherry inside. They both laughed. Suddenly a familiar sound, a terrifying sound. Without thinking, she ordered her brother to run inside the house. The grenade hit the plum tree and exploded. Splinters flew everywhere. She kept running, avoiding every splinter. This was her world. A five-year-old girl forced to call this her home. Still shocked, the little girl stepped outside her house to see what had happened to her family. She saw her brother under her grandfather, whose hand was bleeding. She saw her grandmother in a pool of blood next to the cherries. But she did not cry. It was war and she was used to it. Grenades exploding and seeing her friends die was a part of her life.

It was 1993. The war in Bosnia and Herzegovina turned from bad to worse. After the grenade explosion, the girl's parents had found a safer village in which to live. Hardly any bombs exploded after they moved. On a particular day after school, she was heading home with many of her friends. Close to her house, a fight in a bar had caused many people to crowd around the long road. The children stopped to look. A car was driving along the road. The schoolchildren ran to the other side to follow the fight. The car started to hoot and a loud smash was heard. A child was thrown into the air and onto the ground. The girl stood frozen, afraid, not knowing where her brother was. She felt someone curl around her leg. She finally started to breathe. The dead boy's older brother started screaming, 'My mother is going to kill me!'

The girl's parents had no choice but try to escape the brutality that was thrown at them day by day. The only escape was an illegal transportation to Germany. A few months after the grenade explosion, she found herself sitting in a cold truck, surrounded by unknown people and the smell of naphtha. She was on her way to Germany but terror followed her like her own shadow. She turned towards her mother who always kept herself from crying. Her brother was looking at her. He longed for comfort and the girl gave it to him. Approaching the German border, they were told to be as quiet as possible. The truck travelled at night because the sun would expose their shadows and that would result in death. Hardly breathing, she saw a German soldier approach the truck. He banged a few times on the truck, making sure it was empty. Suddenly an old woman started to cough. All the people around her jumped onto her to quieten her.

She finally did. Her brother's hands were holding the thick truck's bars. She saw, as if in slow motion, the soldier hitting the bar between her brother's hands. How close she had come to death once again. Still, she remained silent because that is what she was used to.

Finally she was in a country where the sound of bombs didn't dominate her mind. But her experiences made her unique and not many people understood her. Even though she pretended that everything was all right, she still had something missing in her heart. She was in a different country. The people treated her without respect and without sympathy. Not that she longed for sympathy. She longed for a place to feel at home, a place to feel safe and wanted. This country did not seem to offer her that. The first day of school was not like any normal day. She felt rejected not only by her new friends but by her own people as well. A seven-year-old Bosnian boy who was accepted by the Germans refused to sit with her. Standing in front of the class she felt rejected by the whole world. However, she smiled and sat alone in the back row. A few days later, a maths teacher approached her. Without any knowledge of the language, she understood him. His eyes said it all. She was not alone. Not anymore.

1995. The war in Bosnia had ended. The little girl had found a new home in Germany. She met Germans who did understand her and started to question the reasons behind her survival. But three years after the end of the war, Germany turned its back on her. She was forced to return back to the country she once called home. To the country that no longer existed in her heart. But soon her state of emptiness ended when Australia offered to provide her a safe home, an education and a reason to live.

> *Once felt rejected by one nation*
> *Forgotten by the world*
> *Never realised what home meant*
> *Until Australia rescued me.*

Australia gave me a home, freedom
Opportunities to be whatever I wanted to be.
Today I stand before you and proudly call
Australia my home.

Standing proud in front of her class, she recites the poem. This time she is not alone. Her friends share the same faith and lived through their own horrors. Her experiences have made her a stronger person. She is not afraid to take chances in order to achieve her dreams. She is not afraid to step out and speak her mind. She does not trust everyone because she had learned that trust can be bought and not earned. In her eighteen-year-old face, a wise woman is reflected.

Last summer she visited Bosnia. The country that she had once called home is now ruined, and with it her most cherished childhood memories. But not the memories of the war. They haunt her wherever she goes. She believes that sharing her experiences will cleanse her of her memories of the war.

The young girl who survived the unthinkable is me. Often I wonder why I survived. I hope it is because I have a purpose in life. I look once more at the sunset and head for home. Who knows, it might be the last time that I see it . . .

My Greatest Escape

by Mert Korkusuz, aged 12

It was cold. Very cold. The waves splashed on my face and the misty air tightened its icy grip around me. Our small boat was crowded with the people I had known all my life. It was terrible. But we had no choice.

We all had a small bag each, half full with our belongings. I had one spare shirt and pants but no warm clothes. I took my one and only book along with a picture of my brother who had recently died in the war. My parents looked many years older overnight when the dreaded news was given to them. Their smiles were wiped off their faces. I no longer see my mother's beautiful smile.

We are escaping from the war. War is terrifying. Young men and women, children die. People lose their loved ones. Innocent blood is spilt. What is the point of war? Why go to war? There is no victorious side in a war. Everyone loses. Some lose their lives, some their dignity. Some lose their hopes for the future, some their humanity. What is the point?

Ali . . . My best friend. Short but solid, fast and courageous. Nobody could catch him. Best runner in the whole neighbour-hood. I miss him already. We spent every day together. We had so much fun in the old days. Poor Ali! He wanted to come with us. But how could we take him? Both of his parents were killed in a bomb attack. My parents couldn't take him. Everyone was trying to save himself. Tears in his eyes as I left him forever are still fresh in my mind, in my heart . . . My best buddy. Forgive me! Forgive me for leaving you behind. What could I have done? Maybe I could have hidden him somewhere in the boat. I feel so hopeless, so helpless . . . What sort of a friend am I? Help me God; help me to come to terms with our misfortunes. I didn't want to leave you, Ali. I didn't want to leave any one of you. We would spend hours along the muddy creek with a hope of finding a little round stone. We would play hide and seek in the good old days. But things were different after the war started. We were not allowed to leave home. How would my poor brother Hassan know that it was for his own sake to stay indoors? Sneaking out one day cost him his life. I wonder how my friends are. How is life treating them? Are they all right? I sure hope so . . .

My home, the one I was born in, is destroyed. I lived there for all my life. Twelve years . . . We had so much hope for the future. I was going to work really hard and become a teacher like Mr Rahmi. Teach children how to read and write. Teach them everything there is to know. I didn't want to be a farmer like my parents. I was going to be the first teacher from my village. Was it all a dream? Am I really going away from home? Where am I going?

It is freezing. The sun is disappearing on the horizon. It is cold. We all huddle together for warmth. I don't think it is making much difference. We haven't had a proper meal for a long time. I am starving. I hope this mysterious journey won't take much longer. I don't think I can take it any more. I feel weak. I feel sick. But I have to hang on. Today is not much different from yesterday. Or the day before. Or the day before that. When will this torture end? Why couldn't we stay home? Why did we have a war? Why did my brother have to die? Why did we have to leave Ali behind? Why? Why? Why? I feel like screaming. I feel like diving into the water and turning into a fish. I feel like crying my eyes out. But I have to be quiet. I look at the sky and pray to God that there will be sunshine in our lives once again. I pray that the thick clouds over our lives will disappear.

I wonder how the new place will be. I overhear people talking about it. They say it is nice. There is no war. Plenty of food and lots and lots of space. The place is called Australia. Very different from my home village, Mum says. They say there are lots and lots of trees in some parts. Some very unusual animals. Animals that hop and carry their babies in their pouches. I wonder if the people are nice. Are they friendly? Are they going to hurt us? Am I going to like it? I wonder if I will be able to have friends. No. No! No place could be as good as my home. I want to go back home . . . But I know it is impossible. Merciless consequences of war.

My mother woke me up this morning with a gentle kiss. 'Our new home' – she pointed out the distant land to me. I jumped out of my seat hoping to see every little detail. 'Calm down,' she whispered. 'There are still hours before we can get there.' All I could see was a piece of land. I could feel the butterflies in my stomach. What if I don't like our new home? I was tired. I wanted to sleep . . .

Hours felt like years. Finally we could see the trees and buildings. Everyone on the boat was quiet. Awfully quiet. I didn't know what to think. At least I knew I was going to be out of this vessel soon. Maybe there would be some food. The motor was slowing down. We were approaching the pier. Who were these men in some sort of uniform, looking at us? I held onto my mum's hand firmly. Someone from our boat was talking to the men. Not a word I could understand. The man from our boat showed some papers to the men in uniform. They looked at the papers very carefully. Everyone was quiet. The men from the boat told us to come out and follow the man in uniform. We did as we were told. My legs were hurting as I walked. Where were they taking us? Finally we made it to the room full of chairs. More talks, more looking. When can we eat? When can we sleep? I was running out of energy. The room was turning around and around.

I opened my eyes. Where was I? Terrible smell . . . 'He is all right thank God,' one woman hurried towards Mum. Why was Mum crying? She held my hand and whispered, 'Please don't leave us, please get better.' Doctors, nurses . . . What was going on? They told me to relax and try to sleep. 'Exhaustion,' the doctor said. Not enough food, not enough sleep and cold nights . . . My body couldn't take it any more.

For days I was in this little room. But at least I was given plenty of food. I felt better by the day. 'You can take him to your room,' our translator told Mum and Dad. I saw them smiling for the first time since Hassan left us. Maybe our new life wasn't going to be so bad after all.

'Is this our home?' I asked Mum. 'But why are these tall wire fences all around here? Can't we go out?'

'We have to stay here for a while,' said Mum. 'Listen,' she said, 'listen carefully. Can you hear any shotguns? Can you hear explosions? This is peace. We must be thankful to God for what we have. We have peace; we have food, clean water, somewhere to sleep. We have each other and we have hope for the future. Let's not worry about not being able to leave this place for a while. I promise you it won't be long before we have our own little home again. I promise you that, you will go to school and become a teacher as you always dreamed. I promise you, we will never have war again.'

I wish Ali was with me. Good night Ali. Hope that one day you can come too . . .

A Bit of My Life

by Sam, aged 15

My name is Sam. I come from Iran. I have been in detention for almost four years. I want to tell you my story.

I left Iran with my family because we were persecuted for having a different religion. Most people in Iran are Muslim, and the government is Muslim too. The government does not like people to have a different religion so we were treated badly. At school the Muslim teachers let the students tease us and we were punished unfairly. We are not allowed to study at university.

My family had to leave Iran because my father was in fear of his life. I was eleven years old and my sister was nine. When I left my city Ahvaz with my parents, we had to pretend we were going out for a day trip, because our Muslim neighbours would tell the police and we would have got into big trouble.

So we went to the capital city Tehran in an aeroplane. I had to sleep at the airport with my family. It was very scary because there were police everywhere watching for refugees. It was also very noisy – loudspeakers loudly calling the flights, loud horrible music and uncomfortable plastic chairs. In the morning we felt very tired and worried about getting onto our plane for Kuala Lumpur, in Malaysia.

We stayed in Malaysia for two weeks in a hotel. We could not speak Malay; we could not speak any English so we had to use sign language. The food was too spicy and hot for me. It was such a different culture that we did not have a happy time there. But we had escaped from Iran.

We went to Jakarta for one day, then we flew to Bali. We were there for four weeks. Jakarta was very big, dirty and confusing. I was happy to leave. I liked staying in Bali. Because I was never allowed to swim in Iran, I tried swimming at the beach and the pool in Bali and I learned to swim! The Balinese were friendly but they always wanted to sell me things I did not want. However I could not relax in Bali, because we had to keep moving every couple of days, carrying our entire luggage.

After that we were going to go in the boat to come to Australia but we had to travel to another city, Teram. So we travelled with the car that time. It took us about four hours to get there. When we arrived, it was about eight o'clock at night, we were very scared and the weather was very hot, and all the lights were out near the beach. We had to get on the boat without the police seeing us because what we were doing was illegal.

So we went to the small boat. It took five minutes to get to that big boat and when we arrived there were not any stairs. We had to climb up and, as I was climbing up, the rope snapped. I was almost falling into the water but someone grabbed me and pulled me up. Then a Norwegian man fell in the water. My mother started to cry because it was too dark to see and she thought I had fallen into the water. As she climbed up she found I was safe. She was so happy.

Everybody was scared the first night. We did not have any food – we went to sleep hungry. On the second day we had some lunch and, as I started to eat, I began to vomit because I was seasick. I could not even move and the third day we had ran out of food because people were eating too much. When the food finished every one started to fight over the water. There was no place to sit or lie down. I fell asleep huddled up in a corridor.

Some people were stealing the water and hiding it. Other people were using the water too. We saw many dolphins and sharks and sometimes the sharks came up to the boat. Everyone was scared and screamed. On the fourth night the sea became very rough and it seemed as though the boat went up in the sky then came falling down. When I was down inside the boat I heard the nails creaking. I thought the ship was opening up. On nearing some islands, we saw a huge ship. The captain of our boat told everyone to duck. They could report us to the authorities. It was very scary!

We were four and a half days on the ocean, then at six in the morning we made it to Ashmore in Australia. The Australian police told our boat to stay put until they returned. Then they said we have to stay in the boat for seven days until the big boat came to pick up the families first. Then the single men were to be transported to Darwin. The police left us just enough food and water.

We were three days in the boat after they came back for us. When we got to Darwin I was very scared. I was wondering what was going to happen to us. Where were they going to take us? They told us we had to get into the bus. So we did. I felt like I was back in Iran with the police hassling me because I was different. They took everybody to a huge gym and two men came in and they started to talk with us about what was going to happen to us. They said, 'We are going to transport you to Woomera Detention Centre after we check you out and your fingerprints.'

It was hard to understand his English, but I knew something bad was going to happen, just like in Iran when the police grabbed my father. I felt really scared, but because I was in Australia, I knew I would not be killed. But I saw a man pass out and fall on the floor when he heard the man in uniform tell us we were going to be locked up. His wife and child started crying and screaming in loud voices. My family was scared too, and my mother was crying. Next the men took away all our things – our money, necklaces, earrings and backpacks. We had only the clothes we were wearing on the boat to Australia.

We left Darwin at two in the morning. We flew from Darwin to Adelaide in a small plane, so we were really hungry when we arrived at Adelaide. It was still dark and we were put straight into a bus. We did not even see the airport building.

We had been on the road from Adelaide to Woomera for two hours. We had another four hours to go and everyone was very hungry. We finally reached our destination, and now all we could see was barbed wire and huge fences enclosing our living arrangements, compliments of the Australian government. Everyone forgot about being hungry and just stared at the sight before their eyes. Some people started to cry. It is hard to explain the feeling you get when you know all your freedom will soon be taken away from you for God knows how long.

We were waiting to get in there for over two hours and people were becoming impatient, but not me: I did not want to be locked away like a caged animal. I wanted to save myself from the horrors that I had left behind. I saw the gate swing open and walked into my uncertain future – we were all huddled together, terrified. We were confronted by a man with a moustache. He started counting heads. When he finished counting, another gate opened and he told us to go inside. In the distance we could see eyes looking back at us. Both gates closed with a loud bang. We found ourselves surrounded by unfamiliar faces. We were shown to our dongas, which were no bigger than a laundry room, and we settled in the best way that we knew.

We then go outside to introduce ourselves to the other people. They tell us how long they have already been here: between one and two years and we are shocked. We thought we may only be here for a couple of months.

We have come to the realisation that we are in detention in Australia, but I have to remember this is just a bit of my life, and who knows what the future holds. Perhaps a new beginning?

A Second Chance:
The Story of Le Hai Nguyen

by Victoria Shaw, aged 11

My mother has been in Australia for almost twenty-two years, and throughout my childhood I have heard fragments of her horrible experience fleeing Vietnam. She often told me that one day I would be old enough to understand and retell her sad story to the world.

One day after school I told my mother an opportunity had arrived for me to write about her journey to Australia. Her eyes then filled with tears of happiness and sadness – happiness because I was interested in finding out about her journey but sadness at the terrible memories of those horrible teenage years. For the first time, she retold that chapter of her life. Later that night, having heard my mother's story, I felt so sorry for her. Coming to this country was a perilous journey and learning a different language as well as supporting herself while studying was a great challenge. Nevertheless, she overcame all these barriers. I am proud that I have a mother who is always determined to achieve everything she sets her mind to; and most importantly, she often advises me that I should always appreciate what I have. This is my mother's story.

I was born in a small town about ninety kilometres south east of Saigon. My parents were middle-class farmers and, even with a large family of fourteen children to support, we had a good life. In 1975, after the Communists took over the South of Vietnam, my family became very poor. My brothers were penalised for serving in the United States Army and put in a re-education camp to learn about Communism and work as labourers. During that time my family was tortured by the Communists and suffered great poverty and starvation. I lived through this terrible time always thinking of a chance to have a good life again.

In 1981, my older sister, who lived in Saigon, arranged for me to escape from Vietnam by boat. The price for my chance at freedom was gold and to risk my life and that of my younger sister who would accompany me.

The arrangement was strictly secret; we couldn't tell anyone – not even our parents. It was heartbreaking saying goodbye to them, with a promise to come home from a visit to Saigon in a month's time – but knowing we might never see them again.

The engine of the boat we were to escape in started up and we began our journey in the dark of night. Suddenly the engine spluttered to a stop; it had broken down. We were so frightened about being captured by the Viet Cong – even some of the strong men left the boat and ran for their lives across the rice fields. Fortunately for us, a young boy managed to fix the engine. We cried tears of relief but decided to go back to the safety of home after our frightening ordeal.

In our second attempt to escape Vietnam, my sister and I boarded a small, flimsy fishing boat in Saigon River with fourteen other desperate people. We were told to lie in the bottom of the boat and were covered by planks of wood to avoid being seen. I remember having to lie very still until we were safely through the Vietnamese zones. Then, we discovered that the owner of the boat had bought broken binoculars and that there was not a map for directions. We panicked but fearfully continued our journey.

After five nights a severe storm angrily tossed our boat up and down making us cold and wet. We vomited so much from seasickness that we thought we were going to die that night. The next two nights we burned our T-shirts to make SOS signals to other ships in the far distance. They ignored us. Sadly we realised that we were heading nowhere and our situation was hopeless. We desperately wished to see a sign of a bird or land, but all we saw was the empty and angry dark sea on the horizon.

On the seventh night, we became very anxious as we ran out of both food and water. In the calm morning, while trying to scoop some seawater to brush my teeth, I touched some dolphins, which seemed to be taking our boat to an unknown place. As I looked up, I saw an object in the far distance. I screamed and cried, 'Please God help us – let a friendly ship come and rescue us.'

As the object came closer it appeared to be a huge American tanker. We were so happy with the thought that they would pick us up and take us to safety. Unfortunately, there was another refugee boat on the other side of the tanker waiting patiently to be helped. I felt so disappointed and my dream slipped away once again. They dropped some food and drinks down to our boat and then showed us the direction to Malaysia.

As we neared the Malaysian border a pirate boat stopped us. Five women, including myself, were told to hide as quickly as we could. Many terrifying stories went through my mind about evil pirates in Thailand destroying Vietnamese refugee boats and killing people, especially women. We hid, terrified, but with our hands ready to beg for our lives. Fortunately, it must have been a religious pirate boat, as it had a cross on top of its mast and they left us alone. What luck!!

Finally, we landed in Malaysia and saw tourists at the beach. They called the police who then came and hesitated to step onto our boat due to its ragged condition. When I disembarked I couldn't stand or walk because my legs were weak. I was so thin and pale and had lost eight kilograms. We were then taken to a refugee camp on an island somewhere in Malaysia.

We lived on the island for four long months. We were bitten by rats and slept on bamboo beds with little food. Finally we were interviewed by American officials who asked us if we wanted to go to America. We had heard that Australia was a better place for women to live.

Finally, in 1982, my sister and I arrived in Perth with just a smattering of English which we learnt in the camp. We stayed and studied English for six months at the refugee hostel. Later in the year, I was fortunately given a place in Engineering at the University of WA. It was an extremely difficult period in my life in Australia. During that time, I constantly faced and over-came many barriers. Apart from battling the difficulties of cultural differences and studying in another language, I had to work as a part-time cleaner, waitress and general hand in a crayfish factory to support my sister and myself. I also often sent money to my family who remained in Vietnam. In 1987, I graduated and was employed by Telstra as an engineer. Despite all these challenges I have prevailed. I have always believed that if you work hard you will succeed. I now have my second chance and call Australia home.

The Russians Are Coming: Ilse's Story

by Jessie Clifton, aged 13

We were very happy there, in the rolling fields of green grass. In the winter I'd watch the children of the village slide down the same hills blanketed in snow. It was called Frankenberg in 1944, in Germany. It was our home. I lived there with my brother Helmut, and my sisters, Renate and Giesela. I was sixteen when the Second World War started between Germany and the Allies. My brother, my father and the love of my young life, Peter, were immediately shipped off to fight for their country. Our country . . .

We spent many a cold night waiting for news from our loved ones at war. The news came to me, but not what I wanted to hear. It was a warm day but suddenly all went cold, as I imagined living my life without Peter, my first true love. Tears came to my eyes as I remembered every detail about him. I shed a river of tears in his memory.

The seasons changed and winter came. The snow fell and the temperature dropped. The children didn't play in the fields this winter; we all stayed inside and thought of our brothers, fathers, boyfriends and husbands. Giesela was at school camp, back that very day, if the bus didn't get bogged. My friend Elisabeth and I were talking aimlessly, as young people do, when Elisabeth noticed a peculiar sound. We froze and listened. Suddenly it dawned on us, a chilling thought: it was gunfire. It became louder. There was no doubt in our minds now. Someone, or many people, had guns outside and they were getting closer.

We leapt out of our seats. What was happening? Why were there guns? We searched for somewhere to hide just as the door burst open. It was a German soldier. He entered, bringing with him a gust of cold wind. Terrified, we huddled together. He looked grim, a cold figure that sent fear right into our souls. And he was on our side. 'Young ladies,' he addressed us, 'you have half an hour to grab anything you can and then we leave.' We sat there, shocked. Why did we have to get our belongings? Why did we have to leave? He answered our thoughts with a grim nod: 'The Russians are coming.'

I ran outside. *Giesela*, I thought. She was still at camp. She should be here soon. We rushed around, frantically grabbing all the belongings we could. I picked up some photos, a change of clothes and a doona to attempt to keep the snow off. My family grabbed a sled and tied our belongings to it, including a change of clothes for Giesela. 'Come on!' I cried aimlessly into the snow in frustration. 'Giesela, please hurry!' Ten minutes and the trucks would leave. *Please*, I thought, *please, please, please*. Five minutes. I heard the gunfire. 'We have to leave!' called a soldier. *No, no, no, no, Giesela, please*. Then finally we saw a school bus. *Thank you, thank you*. Gisela ran out confused. With no time to explain we all piled onto the trucks provided by the German army. We squeezed up next to my friend's family. We looked at each other, cold and afraid. One face was missing from my family: Joseph my thirteen-year-old cousin. I looked around in time to see him being dragged out of our house by a German soldier, screaming about wanting to stay and defend his home from the oncoming Russians. A tear ran down my face as I thought of leaving my home. I looked up and saw the trembling figure of my friends' youngest sister Johanne. I wiped the tear away. I had to be strong.

Every time the truck went over a bump we nearly fell off. For three hours I'd listened to Johanne cry as we clung to the truck. I felt like wrapping my arms around the poor child, possibly to comfort me as much as to comfort her. Then I looked up in time to see in slow motion as Johanne lost her grip, as she slid to the edge, screaming in fright, as her body was dragged under the wheels, as her lifeless corpse was left behind. The first of us to be lost forever.

Three hours later we arrived at Speiznitz. Hungry and exhausted, we were set up in a local school's gym hall for the night. The next morning we would get on a train to Magdeburg; from there we would have to contact the rest of the family to see where we would go.

The next day we travelled by train. The train was crowded; I had to tie the sled to the outside. The doors were left open so that a few more people could squash together. I slept standing as the train moved towards Magdeburg.

As the train came to a halt our hearts broke right there. The town had been bombed. The ash was so thick we couldn't tow the sled through it. We set out through the rubble. We decided to go to a small village not far away from Magdeburg. The only problems were that we were tired and we were on foot. For weeks we battled the ashes by foot. We reached the village hungry and tired.

The war came to an end, but our troubles were far from over. Amazingly my father found us after much searching, but what he told us was too much to comprehend. 'The Americans have decided that Russia will now own this part of Germany. We must move on!' he urged us. No one listened. It was getting cold again outside and we were settled again by now. But my father was right. And the Russians did come.

Germany was divided into two sections. One part was controlled by Russia under the Communist law, and one part, which was 'free', was controlled by America. My father had a sister in Enger, in the west, the free side. We were going to have to cross the border. In the middle of the night we huddled together, very cold and afraid that we would be shot. We waited in the bushes. The guard turned around and we sprinted. I ran faster than I have ever run before. I dived into the bushes first, followed by the others. We had made it. We were across the border.

We arrived at my aunt's in autumn 1945, almost a year since we left our home. Our house now belonged to a Russian family. We never got back any of our belongings, nor did we find out what happened to them. The war and all the hardships it brought on our family were finally over. With nothing left except each other, it was time to start a new life.

We did not have any of our possessions, but we did have our freedom.

Green Valley

by Fernanda Valdés Chepe, aged 19

You calculate a path through the kisses of your fat aunts and cousins into your new kitchen. The time has arrived, as it does every year, for a branch of the family to settle into a new house. You are sure that the family never plans it this way, that they intend staying a whole decade each time, but it seems there's always something better lurking just around the corner, something newer, bigger; and, since those violent arguments between your mother and the neighbours (they had accused her of stealing this time), you really had no choice. Endless waves of bigger and cheaper houses appear each year, spreading farther and farther west. Today you find yourself in an impossibly condensed suburb packed with identical double-storey dreams. A suburb less than two kilometres from your last, designed to excite the new-found freedom your parents are still caught up in, a freedom that has lasted since 1986, still secure and at just three hundred and ten dollars a week. A freedom that is choice and comfort and working-class desire.

You read the nervousness in your mama's eyes, because she's smoking heavier now and keeps mentioning *el gringo*. Imagine coming all this way to find the place too messy, perhaps He won't like the food, or worse still, He won't eat. Consuelo, your sister, is dancing outside in her bikini. You watch the sun explode off her wet skin, creating fireworks down her long, dark legs. If you looked exotic, maybe you too could score a *gringo* boyfriend. You peek down at those short, round, yellow drumsticks you're attached to. You hate their shape. You hate their colour. Your *tia* nudges you to begin on the potatoes. Short, round, yellow potatoes. You hate that sinister native gene that randomly slips into the make-up of innocent Chilean children. You often spot it on the street, at the markets, at the station: a melancholy mirror. You hate your potatoes. Your cousins would torment you as a child with lies of adoption. That you were really the daughter of a Vietnamese couple who were jailed for eating their other children, and their dog. That you were found on a rotisserie naked and smothered in honey sauce. You grin and work a potato as if there's a different colour hiding inside it. Your mama smacks you on the back of the head.

You taste your favourite of the ten salads prepared. Your mouth waters from the smell of lemon. As she exterminates a cockroach, your mama nervously asks Consuelo if there are any at *el gringo's* house. 'Thay don haff food at his hawoose,' laughs your *tia*. Consuelo complains that it's too hot to move to a place with no pool, and why couldn't we get a nicer yard. You stare at the bare, almost nonexistent turf and the view of endless double-storey walls; of concrete sound barriers; a skyline bereft of trees. You had to settle for no lawn this time, 'but if you'd seen the walk-in wardrobes,' well, you'd know it was worth it.

You walk outside onto the hot patio tiles and light your cigarette. The bush-fire air fills your lungs; it dries your nostrils and throat. Your cousins yell and shriek in impressive Castilian; brilliant and crass Castilian. They run in and out of the double garage your parents had to get, because they could do just as well, even better than your *tias* and *tios*.

The men slurp their beer and Bacardi around the barbecue. You imagine them all scurrying across from a land they never mention. Where they had something. Where they were some-body, and where they were magnificent. Those who can will switch to broken English when He arrives, but for now they laugh and become louder, as the smoke slips away into the ebb of the orange atmosphere. Surely His North Sydney sky is not so orange?

It does not bother them that they own nothing. Your spiral staircase sifts away their regret over what little they have been able to recover. And in a curious way their very own ensuite seems to cloud the fact that everything is being swept away from beneath them again, only a little slower this time. That they are not free, they are not secure. That they will never truly feel proud, or satisfied, or unafraid.

You remember the last time He came, the women were unsure whether to kiss Him hello or just nod. You recognised their nervous expressions because you make those yourself some-times when you try your muddled Spanish. The barbecues bring you back to your childhood. To when your only anxiety was of them leaving you at the end of the night; being locked up in your room to face school, alone, the next day. Tomorrow your *tios* will be retelling today's jokes. At work they will be reminded of what they cannot have, and what they must settle for. And slowly, year by year, they grow to accept it. They even appreciate it a little. For after everything – after the battle and the move, after the loss – what is permanence?

The Journey:
Afaf al-Aryahi's Story

by Hope Mathumbu, aged 16

It is 1991 and the town of Basra is still and sleeping. In one middle-class house, I lie curled up against my mother's warm body. I am a small girl of five.

The only thing that matters is my family next to me, both physical and emotional incubator from the coldness the world has to offer. We are unaware of the impending Gulf War. Closer to home is the danger we are in due to my father's involvement in an underground movement to overthrow Saddam Hussein, the dictator who had already spread his iron fist over most of the country.

In one fell swoop, the peace is disturbed forever as our front door comes crashing down and soldiers raid the entire neighbourhood to extract and terminate any informants or threats to the government. I can do nothing but watch and cling to my mother, who is hiding a gun under her skirts. Hiding it away from those who would surely kill us on the spot if it was found.

The next six months we spend with my grandfather.

My father has gone away to Saudi Arabia because he is an English teacher and is therefore suspected of being an interpreter for the American Army.

I know that he is an interpreter.

I would always join my two elder brothers and my sister behind our parents' door in order to learn our fate. One night, my father was showing my weeping mother his black army box and he said to her, 'If you knew what was in here, you would kill yourself.'

After that day, I did not think of disobeying the instructions left by my father not to converse with strangers asking for him – and indeed many of them cornered me outside of school, sometimes bearing gifts. I cannot account for the intelligence or luck that guided an unguarded woman like my mother to survive alone with a handful of naïve children in such perilous times. Love and dedication perhaps.

My father's return from Saudi Arabia does nothing to alleviate our fear. Already, two of my cousins have never been heard from again after accompanying the police for questioning. They came for my father on several occasions. Once, two men in crisp uniforms that cursed the very idea of security delivered a note for him to spend five days of detention for questioning. It was a miracle that he came back.

I remember vividly one of them looking in my eyes as he dragged my father away. I recall clearly even today that which I saw – nothing.

Life among less frequent invasions became normal. But under all the normality, the fear was high and future uncertain.

The next few years my father spent quietly selling off parts of the business and our belongings to gather enough money for us to make our journey to the only possible salvation – the North. It was truly our last shred of hope as it was the only place untouched by Saddam Hussein.

Everyone wanted to go to the North. Making it over the border would be hard because watchtowers had been formed to prevent people from leaving. Everyone woke up quickly to the fact that the government wasn't a good one, but nothing could be done to match the power and brutality of Saddam's regime.

Anyone without the proper documentation would not be allowed to cross the border. Documentation that would never exist if you happened to be on the wrong side and documentation you would soon lose if you carelessly decided to go sightseeing.

Four years were spent implementing this plan. Four years spent with my cherished father. No matter how cautious or secretive he had to be, he still had time for us.

Asleep in his arms, I could almost forget my fears. Almost.

'One day I will teach you how to speak English and you will be a great doctor in a foreign country so you can help our people,' he would say, with utmost seriousness. I would burst into laughter and bury my face in his chest. 'I will stop myself from growing so I can be your little girl forever.'

In 1994, my mother fell pregnant and my youngest brother was born the next year. A month after that, my family, minus my father, were on a bus to Najaf. My father had to stay behind so as not to arouse any immediate suspicion of our early morning departure. Nothing would ever be the same. It was a bus journey to a possible new life – given only if we could overcome death.

My father met us at a hotel a week later and we all drove to Kirkuk where a contact was waiting to help us over the border. I knew the first time I saw him that he was not to be trusted. We had to abandon our car on the highway where we were then to follow our Kurdish guide over the desert. He led the way holding my baby brother and two-year-old sister. The heat was unbearable and the journey would take eight hours, so we were told; but for freedom we would endure. The cool night breeze came as a relief to our tired bodies. Each of us had a bag with relatively all our life's worth. I watched my father clutch his black box. It must indeed be important because he let one of my brothers carry the much heavier suitcase of money we depended on for survival.

My baby brother started to cry from hunger. 'Sshh,' said the Kurdish man, shaking the poor baby. 'They will kill us!'

Too late.

The night sky becomes daylight. I get to view my first deadly fireworks display. There is screaming. From me? From everywhere. All bags are thrown to the side except for the money, and the black box is hurriedly buried by my father. We slide into a nearby trench. As though nothing had happened, the night is again still. My head lifts from the sand in time to see our Kurdish guide run off with my brothers and youngest sister in tow, leaving my parents, elder sister, five-year-old sister Faten and me stranded in the middle of a dangerous nowhere. My mother weeps for her lost children. 'Think not of them,' replies my father tersely, 'but of us, because we don't know the way. Whatever happens, your children are safe.'

We trudge aimlessly over the hot sand for three days. There is no other life form for miles around. No water. No food. No life.

All we can do now is rest in an empty water canal and pray for salvation. There is hotness in my chest rising to the tip of my tongue. I am too hot to sweat.

'I'm going to find water!' my father exclaims suddenly.

'Where?'

'Anywhere. Stay here, I'll be back.'

Father don't go! I am too tired to protest. All I can do is raise my chapped lips to his and watch him wander then disappear into the gold. The last goodbye.

We are now four women in the desert. My five-year-old sister is weeping in my lap. I get the crazy idea to drink from her tears or maybe cry a river myself. Stillness.

'Faten? Faten!?'

No reply.

My shaking hand reaches to tickle her foot.

She is dead. Oh Mother, she is dead!

Unable to breathe. Hollow, with only the smell of death to comfort me.

It is too hot to waste our tears.

We are saved by merchants who had, in their wagon, my father's body. I keep his shirt soaked with blood as a reminder that I needed to get out for him. I needed to make it for my father. We are able to bury him with my sister. It turns out we were only two kilometres from the nearest village. In the same village, our guide had abandoned my siblings.

The next day we make it to Iran. Our safety is guaranteed for the next five years.

We have to grow up fast. We manage to secure a prosperous marriage for my eldest sister, who moves to Sweden. A close family friend obtains passports of Malaysian citizenship.

It is my first time on a plane. The happiness that fills my heart is immeasurable.

There are sixty of us in a small compound. All our money has gone to two Asian men who promise us a three-hour journey to freedom.

Six days. Six days of a clear blue horizon, overshadowed by the horrible stench of poor sanitation and the accumulating bodies of starving people. This had better be worth it.

After days of drifting, we are picked up by a bigger boat and helicopter. A good welcome.

Why though is there panic among the adults? 'Are we here? Is this Os-tra-liya?'

'Shhh!'

We are offloaded onto the bigger boat and the old one is sunk by our uniformed hosts.

I watch my whole life, my father go under the surface. At that same time, my joy is turned into a sinking feeling as I realise that this is not the salvation we had hoped for.

The next six months we spend in the Woomera Detention Centre.

For some reason, my father's words of a new life turned sour with his death. He needed to be with me for our dreams to materialise. I had left him behind somewhere.

We are not treated hospitably by the uniformed men and are hardly allowed to go outside. I hear commotion outside. Thousands of people screaming angry words I cannot decipher. I want to go home.

We left just as quickly as we had arrived. A man with papers ushered us out and onto a van.

We were dropped three days later in a commune with other Iraqi people.

This was freedom.

I began school and experienced a whole new world of beautiful people who felt the same about me. I was accepted, loved and, even though misunderstood, people did not mind to take the time to understand me. With all this new happiness, there was still the underlying knowledge that in this same country, other people in my situation are struggling to be free, wanting to find a home. The more I learned the more I understood. But why couldn't everybody have this?

Why us? Why me?

I was grateful and still am for all the blessings that have been bestowed on our lives.

I am not a doctor. I am not fluent in English. I do not have a father. But I have a nation's dream of freedom and that's all that matters to me. A home is not where you are born; it is where you are accepted. A home is not where you are chosen, it is where you have a choice. A home is not where you will be prepared to fight, but where there is eternal peace and therefore no need for arms.

It is 2004 and the city of Melbourne is still and sleeping. In one middle-class house, I lie curled up next to my husband's warm body. I am a girl of nineteen, delivered unto my present state by a journey of pain, death and horror.

Finding My Roots: Norm Fletcher's Story*

by Kyle Sellick Smith, aged 17

With hesitation and trepidation I considered what path I should follow. My time in this place was over and I needed urgently to find a different way of life. I would rid myself of the material possessions that had ruled my life for so long. I desperately wanted to return to my homeland and be at peace. I knew a long journey lay ahead of me.

I decided to give all my belongings to my closest friend, Cyril, before I began my travels. My plan was to head north towards Arnhem Land – my native land – and find my family from whom I had been separated after I committed crimes against the white man's law. This was a journey of reconciliation and hope for a new beginning.

Thick red dust was everywhere as I began my huge trek across the unforgiving desert. The only way out of my misery was to hitchhike. Countless cars and trucks had passed, each one engulfing me in a sea of red dust. Finally, a white ute pulled up a hundred metres ahead. I sprinted for this opportunity but, as I went to jump in the passenger side, I found the door was locked. I walked cautiously and nervously, with an inkling of suspicion, to the driver's side. He wound down the window slowly and spoke in a sneering, husky voice.

---

* This is a story passed down from Norm Fletcher to his grandson Glen MacNeill, who told it to the author.

'You can ride in tha back if ya want.'

I looked and saw a dead kangaroo with blood seeping from it, washing across the tray in a crimson tide. I turned my back on him and his car.

I began to walk along the steaming road looking at my feet. As I looked up at the disappearing road in the hazy mirage of heat-waves radiating from the earth, I questioned the path I was taking. I turned from the road and headed into the strange yet welcoming desert. I had one last look at the stream of cars flowing along the road and finally welcomed the solitude of the desert. On this journey I must forge my own path, hold my head high and take responsibility for my future into my own hands.

It was coming into afternoon and I was feeling dehydrated and exhausted from the 40-plus degree temperatures. I had no water and was starting to feel delirious. I could not venture on so decided to set up camp and try to establish what could be done to improve my situation. I found a shady hideout under a large cluster of spinifex grass. I was in a land of slumber before I knew it.

I awoke to a sky full of stars, cool and crisp air infiltrating through my ragged shirt. In the distant stars I could make out a figure, a woman, who seemed to be pointing the way. I may have been hallucinating from lack of water but I believed that this mystical woman of the stars was helping me find the path that would lead to my family. So I began to hike through the desert once again, guided only by the stars. I started to wonder if this journey was one of survival or new beginnings.

Storm clouds filled the skies as dawn approached and I could no longer use my guide – the woman of the stars. I decided to rest. I replenished myself with a small, spiky, green cactus that I broke open with a sharp rock. I sucked out its tangy and sour goodness.

Hours passed, along with the storm, and the sun was high. Once again I was starting to believe that I might spend my last days in this hostile environment, alone and deprived of what I set out to achieve.

Up ahead I heard the screams and squawks of a flock of galahs. I stalked them and pounced onto one of their nests where I discovered some fresh eggs. I cracked them open and swallowed the slimy contents raw, leaving me with a refreshing but somewhat viscous taste in my mouth. The flock of galahs scattered, heading beyond my sight. I could feel my stomach churning and grumbling, still hungry for food and in need of water.

Then unexpectedly I saw something that made me feel uncertain yet it was significant to me. Its coat shone luminously in the sunlight and for some reason it gave me a boost in morale. The white dingo that stood before me, with its deep brown eyes, made me feel inferior, yet I knew that this dingo posed no threat. I sensed it would help me with my journey. As I surveyed the wide, open plains I realised that I had no clue what direction I should choose. At first, I underestimated the white dingo's presence. But it knew I was lost and began to lead me to my homeland. It reminded me of a white puppy I had once owned before I was displaced from my land so long ago. The dingo had a friendly and casual approach, licking my hands and legs with its sandpaper tongue. I followed him closely. He had a look of inspiration in his eye, continuously checking on my deteriorating condition.

I felt a cool breath of wind caressing my face, a cool humid breeze in stark contrast to the dry, desert air. Although I couldn't see it in the surrounding haze of heat, I could sense my homeland was drawing closer. I could now make out large willow trees on the horizon and birds swarming overhead, criss-crossing the sky, breaking the silence of the desert.

I was on my last legs, weak but determined. I could hear the sound of a didgeridoo getting louder and louder with every step I took. The dingo began to run with excitement, so I chased him, dragging my weary body as fast as I could.

The dingo vanished along a creek bed up ahead. Then I saw an old lady sitting by the creek, holding a long, shiny spear. She turned towards me and threw her arms into the air, but her face was hidden by the shade of the tree. She stepped out and with an emotional bellow she leaped forward and embraced me in her arms with love and compassion that had been absent since I left this place.

My mother looked at me tearfully and asked, 'How did you find your way?'

As she finished her words I heard the distant howl of the white dingo echoing around us and I replied, 'That's how.'

It was at that point I realised that, although I had successfully conquered the physical phase of my travels, my journey was far from over.

VISIONS
OF HOPE

'Australia - what a cool name for a country!'

Iman Zayegh

'All the misery of the past few weeks compounded
in that one moment of despair. We desperately
begged to be allowed to stay. We had come so far,
prayed, suffered, hoped and despaired, and it had
all come to nothing.'

Caitlin Gardiner

The Unforgettable Moments

by Yusra, aged 14

It was hot, noisy, humid and a bit dark. I couldn't sit or stand but lie on the wet floor and roll side to side. The roof was dripping and I felt like I could lapse into unconsciousness. I had a strange feeling. Sometimes pain rooted all over my body, and sometimes I didn't feel a thing.

For three days, one after another. I looked out of the window on occasion, but it was scary enough to make me look away. It was more of a nightmare than a true event; sometimes the wave would rise higher (and I mean much higher) than our lousy little boat and release its heavy weight on top of us. I could then hear the wood trying to escape from the pressure.

I couldn't believe that we were able to get over these mad waves; it was like they wanted to show us how powerful they were, and we were like a toy that couldn't manage itself.

At those tragic moments, I started to think about life and how I had been living all this time. I was thinking of what would happen if the boat gave up. Would we all die, or would some of us stay alive to tell others what we went through? How terrible it would be to die in the sea somewhere far from our homeland in a place where we would be eaten and no one would ever find us.

But it was useless to just think or remember, so I closed my eyes and tried to imagine that I was home sleeping on my own bed. I could not sleep but did get over my fear.

Suddenly I heard someone screaming. I got up and hurried to the ladder. I was scrambling on four legs because I had no energy left to hold me up any more.

We made it! I screamed inside. It was a dream! I couldn't believe it. I wanted to fly but I didn't have wings. I tried to jump around to express how I felt, but couldn't. All I could do was look; I didn't want to blink to miss even one single moment. It was so beautiful – the island was green and full of life; the sky was clear blue. It was the most beautiful sky I had ever seen. We could see the dolphins, the colourful fish through the clear and colourless sea; the sun was warm and calming. I felt I was born again and had a new life to go on with.

We were then flown from Darwin to Woomera. I didn't know where it was; I didn't care and kept on celebrating my happiness and excitement inside quietly. We arrived but I was shocked. It wasn't what I expected. My happiness ended right there. No longer could I find it, and I haven't been able to since.

We were in a prison. There were no other words to describe it. We were the prisoners. I won't try to explain the conditions there, but it was one of the most painful experiences of my life. We were kept there for eight months, long enough to be sorry for the day we were born.

Vuot Bien – The Search for Freedom: Huong Thi Nguyen's Story

by André Dao, aged 16

A thirteen-year-old girl sits cramped aboard a tiny boat with one hundred and nine other people. One hundred and nine strangers. She is all alone – she has left behind her father, her brothers and sisters, her friends. She is searching for freedom.

Everything was controlled by the government – who, far from creating utopia had created a prison. Even the most basic of staple foods had to be bought at the black market, at exorbitant prices too. Just to stay at someone else's house for a few days, permission had to be given from the local police. Speaking out against the government was unacceptable, often leading to imprisonment without trial or worse – being sent to one of the hard labour camps in the endless jungle. There wasn't even the pretence of democracy – just soldiers barking out orders. Vietnam 1979.

Huong Nguyen grew up in this brutal world. Her mother had died two months after giving birth to her, leaving her father to look after eight children – two boys and six girls. Her eldest sister, Chinh, had to cook and clean after her seven siblings. The second son, Thinh, had fought against the Communists alongside the Americans and the Australians, and had lost a leg on a landmine. And while they struggled to survive as a family, they listened to the stories about the glorious West – wealth, opportunity and freedom.

They only brought enough food and water for forty people. But when the word gets out, there is no stopping the people clambering aboard. After all, if they are turned back, the police will pick them up. But the people who were supposed to bring the extra food and water don't make it. The horizon stretches out – a great blue expanse, promising liberty on the other side. If they could just get there . . .

In 1979, her father gave Huong and her eldest brother, Dinh, permission to try and escape. He hoped that maybe some of his family could have a decent shot at life.

Though only a little child, she knows only too well the risk she is taking. It is not the first time she has tried to escape. The first time she set out from Saigon with her brother. They travelled a hundred and fifty kilometres any way they could – by bus, motorbike, car, but mostly on foot. She remembers most of all the waiting. Hours and hours but it felt more like many lifetimes. Or a single moment stretched out for eternity. Fear on the one hand and boredom on the other. When someone finally did come, they got on a boat and they moved to the other side of the river. There she remembers waiting again. But this time no one came. Then a voice said, 'Stay still. This is the police. You are all under arrest.'

The attempted escape was a failure – everyone was arrested and marched down to the station. There they were asked questions. Where are you from? Where are you going? They accused her of trying to 'vuot bien', escape the country, and threw her in jail.

The boat rocks and sways. It makes the little girl feel sick, but she prefers it to the cell she was in. At least on this boat she can see the horizon. In the cell it was pitch black. The soldiers had taken all her jewellery and money. They forced her to take off her clothes so that they could search her. She remembers how humiliating it was. And how scared she was. She is superstitious by nature – ghosts and devils. In the unquiet darkness where she couldn't even see her own hands, her imagination would take over.

After Huong refused to answer their questions, she was sent to Kiem Loung, a prison purpose built for would-be escapees. It was a hard labour camp, where everyone above ten had to carry rocks from the quarry.

On the boat, she is hungry. But this is not the first time she has starved. At Kiem Loung, they lived on a bowl of rice a day, and they drank the fetid water from the pond. On the boat, just like at Kiem Loung, food dominates her mind. She is lonely. All those strange faces, full of fear, full of hope. They have hardly started when they see another boat approaching them. A VC navy boat. They are ordered to stop and told that they must turn back, before being put in jail. Desperate, the people on the boat hand over everything they have, money, gold, jewellery and watches. The police become a lot friendlier, even giving them more water. Money can buy anything . . .

At Kiem Loung she became so sick that they allowed her to return home. However, she was never allowed to go to school again.

A tiny cup of water each. Just enough for them to live and see another day. But what would that new day bring? All around them now is sea. Home and the coast are no longer visible. The rocking makes some people sick. An old lady is dying. Time becomes hazy – every moment leads up to and away from that cup. But despite her thirst, she is glad to be on the boat. It is better than the deathly sickness she experienced after Kiem Loung, and the musty air inside the house she didn't leave for months.

After four months in her house, Huong's father gave her permission to try again. She felt that she had nothing to lose – not even her young life. After all, what is life without freedom?

They have been out at sea for a couple of days now. A French boat appears on the horizon. They hold up their children and raise an SOS flag. The boat runs away. She knows that surely this was their last hope. Without help, they can't possibly make it by themselves. The old woman is still dying. The skinny thirteen-year-old is still alone.

There is a family on the boat with small children. They have brought some extra food to feed their little ones. Seeing the tiny thirteen-year-old girl, they share some of the food with her. They are her first friends on the boat. The food tastes good after days with only water. Many of the others aren't so lucky. The old woman dies.

Like everyone else on the boat, she is sure she too is going to die. The old woman's body lies just a few metres away. The endless horizon has lost its hope – it is only water again. The splash of the water against the boat merges every individual moment of pain into an endless tide of nothingness. There is nothing left to do but wait to die.

It seems that hope appears when we least expect it. For the skinny thirteen-year-old it certainly does. A huge American oil tanker materialises on the horizon, and this time the ship picks them up. They sink the little boat with the old woman's body still in it. On the ship they eat and drink properly for the first time since leaving Vietnam.

The ship meanders around in the South China Sea. They are awaiting approval to enter the refugee camps of Thailand. She thinks to herself that the hard part is over. Once again the blue horizon beckons . . .

Huong spent a year in the refugee camps of Thailand. In March of 1982 she arrived in Australia.

She is now fifteen and slightly less skinny. She is no longer hungry and no longer needs to fear for her life. But she is still alone in this room with thirty other teenagers. A couple smile when she enters the room. Others glare at her. Most of them simply ignore her. After six months at a special school for refugees, her English is still rudimentary. She finds it difficult to understand what the people around her are saying, but she can sense the undercurrent of discontent all too well.

Huong's eldest brother Dinh had been in Melbourne since December 1981. She arrived in 1982. However, no one knew that he was there so Huong had to stay in a hostel around Springvale.

The other students say that refugees have had it easy. They think it has been a free ride – government housing and tutoring. The refugees work hard, but that doesn't impress the Australians. Their hostility frightens Huong but angers her as well. It angers her because they do not know what it is to starve, or to spend days on a boat, staring at the horizon. They do not know what it is like to be in a pitch black room, far away from friends and family.

Faced with such resentment, she retreats back into the familiar. She makes friends with other refugees, people she has met in the camps, and then at the hostel in Springvale. They are mostly Vietnamese, but they are also Polish, Lebanese and Turkish.

After six months at a special English course in Collingwood, Huong began Year Nine at Richmond High School.

She experiences what the other Vietnamese girls call 'ky thi' – racism. 'Ky thi' is the coldness in the way people speak to her. It is the way the Vietnamese are treated as stupid and ignorant, just because they don't speak the same language. It is the glaring, the discontent, the fact that no one cares that some of these people have seen family members die to get here. It is the two groups that form, white and non-whites. It is the fact that she can't go to the toilet alone out of fear.

Some of them blame her for the war in some obscure way. In many ways, she realises, the West doesn't live up to its high reputation. But she is not reproachful: she is too grateful simply to be here. Despite the isolation and segregation, she still feels lucky. She is still surprised by freedom everyday. Even in the refugee camps they were given only a bowl of rice a day and a can of fruit. Here there is food and clean water, yes, but most of all there is a future.

Two years after starting at Richmond High School, Huong transferred to Richmond Girls' High School. Things were better – there were fewer Vietnamese and somehow that made a big difference. Here she made her first Aussie friends, went on her first school camp and discovered the little freedoms she had never known.

The realisation comes as a shock, but she takes it in stride along with everything else that has been thrown at her in her short fifteen years. The horizon that she had yearned for on the boat – getting to Australia wasn't that horizon. It was merely the first step towards it. The horizon, she realises, still beckons. Looking, she sees that the sky is so very blue.

The Confession of a Closet Racist

by David Maney, aged 18

Where does this closet racist narrator begin? Do I begin by telling you that it's not my fault I'm racist? Surely you wouldn't believe that, but I will tell you all the same. On January the 11th I was born into my white Anglo-Saxon skin, the proud son to my white Anglo-Saxon kin. All my life extremists, racists, homophobes and the religious have surrounded me. In short, my whole life I've lived in a country town somewhere out there in that beautiful landscape of middle-class Australia. I knew from an early age that wogs played wogball, the Abos sniffed petrol from tins and all Arabs were terrorists. Despite all the evidence against, these are still the views I have embedded in my genes. Because racism is hereditary. I'm resigned to the fact that the best I can be, despite my best efforts, is a closet racist.

'Hello, I'm David.' I didn't dare put my hand out for him to shake it.

'Hello, I'm Carlos Batres, your gaming attendant for this evening.'

'What?'

The words had flown off his tongue, riding the wave of his rapid-fire Spanish accent that made every word melt into the next.

'David, I'm Carlos, the gaming attendant.'

He dragged my name over a long elaborate thought, holding onto the *a* far longer than anyone ever had. My new boss had told me to be careful about Carlos's flirtatious manner, in that typical closet racist way of never saying anything but implying everything.

Despite Carlos's diminutive stature, we look very much alike: short black hair, similar coconut brown tans gained from a fruitful summer. But I stress this right from the outset: we're nothing alike. I'm the cocktail barman; he's the gaming attendant. We share the same space once or twice a week but share no common ground.

Instantly, I knew that Carlos Batres was gay. It wasn't hard to pick – he was only a Carnevale costume away from the Mardi Gras, such was his unashamed campness. (Oh the cheap homophobic thrill I get from the fact that my computer spellchecker doesn't recognise the words *Carnevale, Mardi Gras* or *campness*.) And it wouldn't surprise you that racists are also staunch homophobes: the formula to concoct racism is not dissimilar from the one needed for homophobia. You need one part ignorance, two parts stupidity and the grated zest of thick skin. Where the racism recipe differs is that it only requires a dash of mob mentality, whereas homophobia requires a splash, a swig, and then another half bottle added to the mix.

You'll be happy to know that this closet racist narrator was alarmed by how much he found he had in common with Carlos Batres. I had never really thought that such similarities could be drawn between us: I had never looked past my knee-jerk reactions before. It suddenly occurred to me, while making a vodka martini, that I too am in the minority; that I too have been harassed most of my life. Despite my surroundings, I have been raised to be an intellectual, instantly springing me into the trap of being in the minority. I am a person who values his opinion. Carlos is a person of race, of different sexuality, and, along with people of gender and of weight, we fit nicely into a group of people who are far too easily pigeonholed by society. But I'm so pathetic and weak that I'll subscribe to any form of behaviour that diverts the eye of segregation from myself. Now, you may or may not be aware that the modern version of the Klu Klux Klan is the male sporting team on a pub crawl, each individual fuelled by cheap liquor, spurred on by his narrow-minded peers. I know it's horrible to generalise, but the smartest of the group (if I wasn't behind the bar this would probably have been me) will always make a joke about Carlos' accent. This man, I suspect, is a closet racist himself. This is all in good fun of course; never, not even for a moment, will a serious tone show up in his voice. So jovial is his manner that everyone laughs along, including Carlos, including myself, but the last laugh is his, that man at the bar, and the last laugh is not with Carlos, it is *at* Carlos.

Most of the time I consider myself a closet racist. But just because I'm alone with my thoughts and I don't share them doesn't make them any better. Just like a closet gay, I have these thoughts and I don't act on them. I cover them up but that doesn't mean they weren't formulated. Their existence is only three seconds away from being off the tip of my tongue and out into this racist world. This doesn't make them any less powerful or any less unsettling for this narrator of yours. I know my true colours and they're not a pastiche of sugar-coated rainbow colours, but haphazard paint strokes of metallic grey, black and blood red, streaked across a stark white background. I'm almost more immoral and more loathsome than that gentleman at the bar, because I know my behaviour is crude and wrong, yet the words are there anyway.

Racism. The word seems to slither off my tongue, my pronunciation highlighting the snake in the grass that I am. It is a sad indictment on me, your closet racist narrator, that I could not for the life of me spell the very word before I wrote this confessional piece. The slippery *s* finding its way between the *a* and the *c*; the gap between what I know is considered politically correct and what I still think, day in, day out.

When I first started asking Carlos questions about his past, my teeth must have shone like a shark's. My subconscious longed for a piece of personal information to pin him down with. In his abstract English he told me the facts of his life, his birth and re-birth (coming out) in San Salvador, El Salvador, a place I knew only because I had seen a snippet of war footage in Michael Moore's film *Bowling for Columbine*. He told me about the civil war that raged for years before he chose to leave his country. *Chose*, because he wasn't a political prisoner; he wasn't newsworthy. He was stuck in a civil war where people were fighting the past and all its flaws for a better future. I would never see the story of Carlos Batres on the news because the situation would never change for him or for the country – everything seemed to stay the same. And it makes me chuckle, quite innocently, to think of Carlos Batres prancing around at the age of fourteen having to complete his compulsory military training. Yes, I think it is safe to say that military training would not have agreed with Carlos.

Unlike Carlos I have no indicators of my upbringing. Only a few colloquialisms that are easily got rid of. His baggage is a burden compared with my carry-on case. He came to a country not knowing the language, a barrier that he thought was the greatest. I'm sure he must know that people like me are judging him, judging his initial inability to fit into the jigsaw of western culture. Without language he was nothing – for once, dear reader, these are his words not mine. The simple act of catching the train was impossible, further hindered by the fact that he couldn't ask for help. And if I were a complete stranger that night he caught the wrong train home, would I have helped him? I fear I might not have, or would only have done so because I despised his pathetic kind so much that I didn't want to be bothered by him. Someone did help him that night and he found his way home eventually. Yes, dear reader, there are far better people out there than this despicable human being whose words you read.

But it was the strangest experience for this closet narrator to find Carlos Batres' story touching. My once cold heart thawed temporarily, lifting a large dead weight, which I suspect is guilt, off the bottom of my rib cage. It is discomforting to have a void of hatred missing within myself, a long-time friend absent temporarily.

Now don't think this is a back flip from your closet racist narrator, but Carlos has become one of my closest friends. That doesn't mean that I won't despise the drunk Aboriginals on the street who, if and when I gave my money to them, would waste it on more booze. I will not stop raising my eyebrows at the pretty boy wogs who wax, moisturise and exfoliate. No, indeed.

For into the multicultural society we like to call Australia is inbred a culture of racism. At the end of the day racism is less about being black and white, or in the case of Carlos and me, varying shades of chocolate brown, than it is about culture. My kind has been raised with racism in their veins – we are a culture that holds fondly and secretly to its heart the fear of change.

Dear Reader, I no longer need to hide in my closet – I have exposed myself.

Surrealistic Nightmare

by Najeeba Wazefadost, aged 16

Leaving your country is one of the most important decisions a human being can be forced to make. It means a break with all that one knows about living – how to earn a livelihood, how to fit in to a society, how to respond to a landscape, how to touch, smell and taste. Every human lives with the images of childhood; for the refugee only memories remain. Sometimes they are replaced by visions of hope for a new world that offers a better way of life. Even if the change to a new way of life is successfully managed, the shock of loss remains.

We come from the destroying enemy. We have come among you in Australia to seek homes or places where we will be safe from the barbarisms of the accursed foe. How sorrowful will be our or any other refugee's position. How desolate their hearts. We refugees have learned by sorrow and distress our dependence on human sympathy. All over our bountiful country the cries of the hungry and the prayers of the needy are echoing.

I AM A REFUGEE. The refugee is a kneeling person, kneeling in front of the captain of a ship to ask for a reduction of their escape price, kneeling in front of the international organisation to ask for their fortune. The refugee's social distinctions, wealth, power, social function, have collapsed completely and evaporated like smoke.

What is left? A human being without any mask. What makes

a person sure and secure but their culture and social identity? A refugee is a person who feels that they are unstable, insecure, and this can clearly be seen in their attitudes.

For the refugee there is nothing that is more important than to live in another country as soon as possible, to get out of the refugee condition and obtain again the prestige and rights of citizens.

And so began a surrealistic nightmare that has virtually no parallel in my life. I suppose the reason for our leaving goes back to when I was eleven or twelve years old. I don't have any attractive or amazing memories of my childhood to wind them back again.

My family and thousands of other families were in danger and persecution from the blood-thirsty Taliban. Because of the very long period of war in Afghanistan, the country was destroyed and it was very hard to live there. All the people who manage to escape persecution and war in Afghanistan pay a very high price. I, in the generic state of being female, was in danger, so also my sister and mother. I didn't have the right to get educated. In Afghanistan girls and women are denied education, health and employment outside the home. We should have had freedom of movement and a measure of respect as individual human beings but this was not the case, in fact we were prisoners of our sex.

The most horrific sound that I have heard during my childhood is the screaming of innocent children, the crying of mothers near the corpses of their children and the dirge of widows for losing their husbands. It still whispers in my head. They killed any people they wanted like animals. Animals might even get killed better than them. Sometimes they killed a whole family together – that was lucky for them because they could die near each other. The Taliban said, 'if we kill by gun, we waste our bullets and it is very dull if we don't kill someone every day.'

They violently raped girls and women which ended in suicide and anguish. I will never forget the doleful day when I lost my best mate. One day I and my dad went to get Mum's medicine. On the way back I saw my friend's dead body in front of the door near our house. It was so horrible to see her unclothed. She was sexually harassed and raped. Her mum was shouting, screaming and hitting her head with her hands. I was sure my friend didn't want to live in this unfair world anymore. She couldn't wait for a better and peaceful life with equal rights. We were always coming to meet each other at the rooftop. I could feel her empty space in my heart.

I was always wondering to myself: are we born to carry all this suffering? Why can't I be like my granddad and go out and fight for my country? Why did God put such a difference between men and women that I had a fear of going out? This probably was the reason that most parents loved to have a boy child.

My family were under so much threat and risk. I didn't know how long I would be alive and live in this unlikely earth. Every second, minute and hour, it was somebody's turn to die and it could be my turn at any time.

OH WHAT A HOPELESS LIFE! Everywhere was terrible – the Taliban were attacking and bombarding houses. I wish it was only the fear of the Taliban but there were so many other dangers – like being a member of the Hazara ethnic group.

So we decided to leave our homeland and get to a safe country. I went to say goodbye to my friend. I told her that she was lucky that she got out of this condition. I told her to ask God when this war will end. I told her I'll never forget the days we had at the housetop. And then I started to cry as much as I could. I thought it was getting late, so I came back home.

I saw everyone ready and waiting for me. My sisters and brother were crying. I thought they were crying because of leaving everyone and our homeland, but this was wrong. My uncle was killed. Yes, one more family increased on the average of widows. I couldn't believe it. My tears just came out of my eyes.

We left our country. It was hard to travel without any transport. It was hard on my mother, who was pregnant. We didn't have enough food to survive. My little sister was thirsty all the time. We didn't have any clue where we were going. Our smuggler told us the best country, which has equal human rights and welcomes us all, is AUSTRALIA. He told us Australia is one of the most amazing countries that we can go to.

We arrived in Indonesia by airplane which was a very frightening journey – at any time we could have been arrested. The time was getting close for my mum to give birth to her child. Suddenly one night I heard my mum needing help. We had to get her to the hospital. We were strangers in the hospital; we didn't know the language to tell the doctor about my mum. So she had to wait for half an hour for my dad's friend to get to hospital to do the translation. At last she gave birth to the child. I heard a baby crying. I saw my new little baby brother. I felt so alone for not sharing that happiness with my relatives in Afghanistan. Unfortunately my mum had a Caesarean. She was tired and looked very weak. The doctor told us she had to rest at least twenty days, but after nine days she had to get up otherwise we would miss the boat. Our boat was so small and disgusting. There wasn't any space for my mum and the baby to sit. Everyone on the boat was looking frightened. I was so scared. All the people were vomiting, including me. I was so sick. I should have taken care of my mum but she was taking care of me. After ten horrible days in the boat and after several rejections of an Australian navy ship we arrived to Australia.

OHHHHHH . . . this is not Australia. Australia is a country which will welcome us. This is a jail. My dream is not that I should find myself in the middle of a desert, a place with wire fences all around and soldiers with guns. We were coming with heaps of hopes to Australia – but we were disappointed.

The detention centre was a place where all refugees were kept for several months and years. I think that asylum seekers flee their country because of persecution and danger – they shouldn't be kept in a locked detention centre. We were coming to get protection – not detention. We came to get freedom. We were locked in detention centres, treated like criminals for no reason. The detention centres are really punishment centres for non-existent crimes. They should be closed down.

People in the detention centre, especially the children, were really depressed. People in the detention centre commit suicide and are in anguish (the same thing that was happening in my country). Children were getting mental illnesses. Our hearts were chastened with hopeless and sad feelings. I and my family were lucky – we only stayed there for two months.

Those of us who were lucky enough to be eventually released from detention found that we still did not receive our right to freedom and security. We were given Temporary Protection Visas, which put our lives in limbo for even longer. Temporary Protection Visas extended our suffering. We were sent to Tasmania and then we came to Sydney because of my parents. We loved staying in Tasmania but my parents were really sad, worried and bored. So we came to Sydney because we heard that my parents could meet some people from Afghanistan so they could communicate with them. It was very hard to settle into the community properly and make a new life for ourselves and our family when we knew we could be deported at any time.

We, and all other asylum seekers, risk our lives to get out, and now we have to survive in a totally different society, with a different language, different culture, separated from family and friends. We all came with hopes for a life of peace, freedom and dignity.

After waiting nearly four awful years without knowing our future, we were granted a Permanent Visa on the 18th of June 2004. And right now I am studying Year Ten. I will try my best to get good results and get into university to study medical science and be a professor. I would also love to be a politician. I will show to Australia that by accepting me in their country I will repay them back. I will contribute to make Australia a better country.

I hope that the policy on refugees will change, because refugees' rights are human rights. I hope that we will achieve equal rights about everything such as women's rights.

A Man in Green

by Henry Upton, aged 14

Have you ever read a poem called 'Men in Green'? It was written by a chap named David Campbell in 1944. It was recommended to me by my English teacher one day through a scribbled note at the end of one of my assignments. *Find a copy of the poem, 'Men in Green' by David Campbell, Henry.* That night I hooked onto the internet. I wondered what could make the poem so good. I punched the title into the search bar and pressed 'enter'. Up came a list of sites and I clicked on the first I saw.

> *Oh, there were fifteen men in green,*
> *Each with a tommy-gun,*
> *Who leapt into my plane at dawn;*
> *We rose to meet the sun.*

I sat up straight in my chair and leant forward, my nose close to the screen. I stopped every now and then to read and reread. After I had finished I sat there for a time, thinking. I knew it had been about the Second World War; about the suffering that Australians had gone through in the jungles and plains of New Guinea. But this human torment is not what touched me. For you to truly understand, I must tell you a story once told to me. A story about a young man named Bob Upton, or rather Sergeant Bob Upton. A man who, in the recklessness of his youth, joined

74

the Australian Army during the Second World War. A man who fought in New Guinea. A man whose story is worth telling.

The three young children lay on the carpet with their hands cupping their chins, their legs lolling in the air behind them. Six bright young eyes stared up enthusiastically at a grandfatherly figure, seated in a big brown lounger in front of a television. It was raining outside and the children had been hurried into the shelter of the house by their parents. The old man stared down at them lovingly.

'Tell them about the war, Dad,' said a dark-haired man as he sat down on a chair with a cup of coffee. 'The little tackers would love that.'

'Yes, I'm sure they would,' said the old man to his son. 'I'm sure they would.'

He settled back into his chair and looked up at the ceiling.

'Yeah, I'd like to hear about that too, Bob,' said a young woman, as she sat down on the lap of the dark-haired man and giggled.

'Yes, all right.' The old man let out a deep sigh. 'I suppose I really should tell you. Well, where to begin?' He sat there for a moment thinking, wracking a brain full of seventy years of memory for a specific point.

'Ah, yes,' he said. 'The German war machine had been growing steadily for the past five years. Hitler had been taking over more and more of Europe as time went on. Robert Gordon Menzies, the Prime Minister of Australia at the time, was forced to act, as our allies were struggling to survive. I was still at school when I first heard that Australia was declaring war. I had been sitting there by an old radio in my parent's house, a boy no older than fifteen. I was so eager to join the Air Force that I tried out when I was only sixteen years old. But I was turned away because of my poor eyesight. Then, disappointed, I joined the Home Guard. Two years later, when I was eighteen, I was called upon to fight in New Guinea. So I left my family and friends in Adelaide and flew to Darwin. I then caught a ship (the *Katoomba* I think it was) to Port Moresby. I remember being so excited about it. On the trip over, most of the young men there (including myself) thought that we were all going to defeat the Japanese in one day, then come home as heroes. We didn't know any better!' The old man took a sip of his coffee and relaxed for a moment, pondering his next thought.

'Well, I was waiting for an assignment at Townsville, when it was noticed that I was one of the few men who could read a map and fire a rifle with skill. My father had taught me that. So I was asked to join ANGUA (collecting intelligence).'

'You would basically just collect information on the Japanese, no fighting or front line stuff!' said the colonel.

I said, 'I'll think about it.'

'YOU'LL WHAT!!' he screamed at me. So I decided to take the offer. No fighting looked like a better prospect than most. I would go on patrols out into the jungle, between command posts, collecting any info I could find. But the only problem was that my patrol was made up entirely of native New Guineans, Fuzzy-Wuzzy Angels as we called them. I was the only soldier in the lot. So if we got into any situation where we had to fight back, we were basically buggered. I swear there was not a man in my patrol who could hit that chair with a standard rifle if his life depended on it.' He pointed towards a high-backed stool in the kitchen no further than fifteen feet away.

'What, so the natives were useless then, Dad?' asked his dark-haired son, making a point to the children.

'Oh, strewth no,' said the old man, shaking his head. 'If it weren't for them we would have been in a right mess, I can tell you. They knew every path, river and valley in the goddamn place. They also carried all of the supplies and the stretchers for the wounded. If I didn't have a few natives with me on the patrols, I would have been lost or dead before the end of the first week. They also let us sleep in their huts during the night. The only problem was that we often didn't make it to those villages. We'd have to sleep beside the tracks. Now that was bloody awful. You didn't know whether a Jap patrol was going to come through during the night and kill you while you slept. We didn't know whether they were going to come through during the day as we walked along the trail either. Oh God, I remember the conditions we lived in. Worse than animals, I tell ya! The weather was hot as hell and bloody humid as well; you only ever got a few hours sleep a night and you didn't take your clothes off for two weeks straight. All you ate was some canned rations and a little coarse bully beef. But if you got something bad like scrub typhus or amoebic dysentery, which a lot of blokes did, you were finished. Basic things like antibiotics were hard to come by; more men died of infection and disease than from bullet wounds. And if you did get sick there was no way anyone could carry you to the nearest hospital or base camp, the jungle was just too thick.'

He leant back. 'But the things that really stick in your mind are the close calls. One time, my patrol was walking past a mill just outside a port held by a platoon of Australians. One of the men travelling with me thought it would be a good idea to check out what was inside and see if there were any rations of food. I told him that we were already a day late and we didn't need to waste more time. When we arrived at the port I was told that Japanese soldiers had been holed up in that very mill we'd walked past. I couldn't believe how close I had been to ending up dead; it scared me so much that I had to sit down for a minute.' He chuckled.

'How long were you there for, Bob?' asked the young woman, a look of deep respect on her face.

'Three years, Cath; I still remember when Japan decided to pull out of New Guinea. It was my twenty-first birthday, and I was stationed at Aitape. I was sitting there right by the radio when they announced it, there was a great cheer from the men around me and I thought, well thank you very much – that's it, I'm off. I went straight to my commanding officer and asked to be sent home. I told them they didn't need me any more.

My dad was pretty ill at the time and he agreed. So I set off on a plane back to Darwin. It's funny, when I got home I couldn't walk down the street without some bugger coming up to me and wanting to shake my hand; this was when the war was still being fought in Europe. People stood aside for me to go through in a queue and things like that, especially when I was in uniform. But it was an entirely different story when the war in Europe was declared over. I couldn't get a job anywhere. There wasn't a bastard who wanted to know me, not my friends, not anybody. I suppose it just sort of went out of fashion. One second everyone treats you like a hero and then the next they don't give a damn. I was spat on once, the Great Australian Spirit, how about that!'

The adults were all shaking their heads.

'No place like home, huh Dad?' asked the dark-haired man.

'Nope son,' he replied. 'There's no place like home.'

My grandfather is Bob Upton. He fought the Second World War in the thick jungles and kunai grass of New Guinea. He spent three years of his life enduring some of the most vile and loathsome conditions imaginable. He did this to keep Australia safe. But when the war ended Australia paid little respect for the suffering or enduring spirit of these men. The people did not care what their own soldiers had gone through. These days we look at war veterans with sympathy, but still not with pride. So if you see an old man, his uniform spotless, with his head held high as he marches in the ANZAC Day Parade, don't try to understand why he does it, and don't think up a reason. Rather just think of what he went through and of those who never made it home.

And I think still of men in green
On the Soputa track,
With fifteen spitting tommy-guns
To keep the jungle back.

David Campbell

Target Practice

by Darko Djukic, aged 18

It was the month of April in 1999. I had just had my thirteenth birthday on the 1st of April but it wasn't a particularly happy one. I was supposed to be in Australia on the 26th of March and, since the bombing of Yugoslavia had begun the day after that, all flights had been cancelled and there was no way possible for my family and me to leave the country. I remember the disappointment that I felt when I found out that we could not catch our plane and that we had to wait for the bombings to stop. My heart broke into a thousand pieces because I began to think to myself that I would never be able to have a free and happy life without having to worry about getting killed. I had already been through two civil wars and yet another one was on the verge of breaking out. My mother was trying to hide her tears when she took in the news from airport security but she was never good at hiding them. The Immigration Department told us to simply go home and wait for further notice. And so we did.

On the 27th of March, in the morning, everyone was already awake before me and the air was so thick that I found it difficult to breathe. I guess I was scared of what was coming our way. At around midday, the warning sirens began to wail and they sounded like screams of the poor innocent civilians about to be killed. I was very frightened but we soon found out through the television that only the military airports and bases were being bombed – not civilians. This gave me a bit of a relief but I was still very afraid. I always knew that something was wrong by the look on my mother's face. Besides knowing the danger of the NATO bombings, I also knew that there was a danger present because my mother looked absolutely horrified. The warning sirens went off again, this time to indicate the attack was over.

That evening, we watched the news, which indicated that everyone should go to a bomb shelter because there was a possible danger of houses being bombed. Since we were staying at our uncle's house, he made the decision that we should all go to the basement because that was the only shelter we had. So we made our way down to the cold, dark and damp basement, which didn't improve my confidence one single bit. I knew even then that if just one bomb dropped in a ten-metre radius of the house that we would be all dead so it made no difference where we were. The dreadful sirens began their screaming again. Not even ten seconds after the sirens started, we heard a loud explosion nearby and my cousin screamed, which scared everyone. My uncle had switched off all of the lights in the house just so we wouldn't attract unnecessary attention. Despite the darkness, I could see the horror in everyone's eyes. More loud explosions, even closer than before. Everyone started to panic because we all began to think that the civilian buildings in the area were being bombed. My uncle, who was a very big man, looked like a ten-year-old boy before his mother when he did something wrong. The fear in him was obvious. These explosions were going on for hours and each of them brought more fear into our hearts. After around two hours, the explosions ceased and once again, the sirens wailed to indicate the end of danger.

We got out of the basement and went back upstairs to see if there was any news on the television. We saw images of burning civilian buildings in the side of the city closer to the military bases and the bases themselves in ruins. Then we realised that our uncle's house was located around ten kilometres from a military base. My mum decided that it would have been better for us to stay at our godfather's place in the centre of the city of Belgrade. So in the morning, we packed our things and said our goodbyes and we headed for Belgrade. We arrived and settled in the house when, once again, the danger alert was sounded. This time, we did not go to a shelter because we figured that the centre of the city would not be bombed because there were only civilians around and no chance of anything military nearby. In the evening, all the adults watched the news and then I realised that they must have heard bad news since everyone looked as if they were looking for something that they couldn't find. I asked my godfather what was happening and he simply replied that we were in danger because our building is right next to the television station, which was being bombed the same night. Everyone panicked and did their bit to make sure that there were no windows uncovered, and moved all the beds into rooms which had no windows.

It was getting late and still there was no sign of the attack warning and I was getting very tired. I had started to doze off when the attack siren woke me up. As soon as the siren was heard, everyone was on the floor covering their heads. After a few explosions in short intervals, which seemed to be far away, I heard a whistling sound in the air which pierced through all the other noises. Shortly after it, there was an enormous explosion which shook the floor and broke windows in the surrounding buildings, and the building that it hit started to crash down. It seemed as if there was an earthquake and for a second I began to think that our building was hit. That thought was erased from my head once the shaking stopped. Not long after that, the entire attack was over. I suppose that the bombers had done what they intended to do. We turned on the national channel and it didn't seem to work. Every other channel was still working. We heard that the television building had been destroyed and we were also able to see the rubble of it from the balcony. All of the following bombings were farther away from us and there was no need for any precautions.

The following month was spent under bombs and anticipation. On the 17th of April, our family was contacted by the Immigration Department and we received good news. We were told that within a week's time, we would be catching a bus to Hungary where we would be met by Immigration officials and receive all the plane tickets and necessary papers to complete our journey to Australia. I spent the following week calling up friends and family that I wanted to say my last goodbyes to and buying things for the journey. Even though all of these horrible things were happening to my country, I still loved it and knew that I was going to miss it very much.

On the day that we left my country, it was unusually cold for the end of April. Spring was finally beginning and the snows were over, but it was really freezing. When the Immigration officials made sure that everyone was present, everyone got onto the bus and we said our final goodbye to the country we could no longer call home. I said goodbye to my family and also waved to them as the bus was leaving. Everyone at the bus station was crying. The people who were joining us on our trip looked as though they had mixed emotions. It was quite hard to tell how they felt because I could sense fear as well as anticipation in the air. The bus ride was only meant to last an hour and a half to two hours but due to customs on the border of Hungary, it took much longer. Since all of my family's bags and papers were checked, we sat down at a table to have something to eat. We could still see Yugoslavian soil. I wasn't trying to look but there was something that caught my eye. I saw a big line of fire tearing the sky into two halves and making a horrific noise as it was coming down closer to the ground. The only bridge that was leading into Hungary and was functioning at the time was blown up into a million pieces. Everyone around us had the same expression on their face and it was as if their expressions were trying to say, 'My God, if we were just ten minutes late – we would have never made it!' The explosion scared little children and brought along a lot of crying which created panic among everyone. That was the last violent image that I have of my country. I have seen many more as a young boy, but those are fading as I get older.

My Journey to Australia

by Lazar Stamenkovic, aged 8

Hello, my name is Lazar and I am eight years old. I come from Serbia. I had to leave Serbia because there were bombs and lots of aeroplanes. One aeroplane nearly hit our house. My sisters were scared but I was not because I had a water-gun, rocks and sticks. An aeroplane crashed near our house and I threw rocks at it. They made little (•). Some people were killed but we were not. My friend had a broken arm from a bomb and I helped him.

I came to Australia in an aeroplane. We ate ice-cream and went to sleep on the plane. Someone gave us Australian money. I threw up on the plane. I was a little bit scared going down in the plane. It was going bump, bump, bump, bump. My uncle came to pick us up. He brought us chocolates, ice-creams, coke and chips. There was loud music playing in the car. We were looking for kangaroos and we saw a baby koala. My sisters were scared of the animals.

First we lived with my grandmother and then we found a house. My dad found a friend from this country. I felt sad when I came to school because I had no friends. Nobody would play with me. In Serbia we would fight and hit with sticks, but in Australia we can't.

My best experiences in Australia are playing with my friend Andrey and playing soccer.

My Baba's Journey:
Katherina Selinski's Story

by Nastassia Allen, aged 15

Would you be able to leave the one place you know as home – forever? Could you survive months of trudging through snow and ice, without the certainty that you would be safe and secure in the end? Would you have the ability to learn a new alphabet, language and way of life – facing racism and trying to hold onto your old traditions?

My grandmother, Katherina Selinski,was only my age, fifteen, when she had to flee the Ukraine with her family and the clothes she was wearing to escape the clutches of Stalin and Adolf Hitler in the Second World War. The horrors that she experienced before she reached Australia strongly contrast the life that I lead now.

Katherina lived a typical country life in Southern Ukraine, near the seaport city of Odessa. Her parents, Basil and Martha Stojcenko were hardworking and productive farmers with a close-knit family. Katherina had three siblings; her older sister Lydia and younger brothers Victor and Alexander. Basil's parents lived next door and gave a helping hand, working hard on the farm. The only water supply was a well in the middle of the town, which was a very long walk from their house. Katherina and Lydia usually carried the water to and from the well in rickety, heavy buckets. Lydia also acted as a second mother to Victor and Alexander. The winters were bitter and their animals had to sleep in the house. Although it was a hard life, the four children attended the local school and frolicked in the forests when they were not busy. The harsh winters also had one advantage – the thick snow gave them perfect conditions for skiing and tobogganing, even though the skates and sleds they owned were mainly made of scrap timber assembled roughly and their clothes were worn and thin rags. 'My sister and I used to sew the seeds and play in the garden. It was exciting because we had no television or Playstation,' she recalls. Animals and friends gave the children most of their fun. In the small field they owned, Katherina used to put their pet duck in the dam and the fluffy, innocent ducklings would follow, their tails wiggling happily. Katherina owned a very young cow – 'white, completely white. Gorgeous,' she smiles. Her name was Taya and she used to follow Katherina everywhere, like a best friend.

What may have seemed a simple and happy life was shadowed by a darkening cloud of fear. Before Katherina was born, it was announced that the ruthless dictator Stalin had taken over Russia. By her fourth birthday, Basil was called out to do hard labour in dangerous mines, three hundred kilometres away. He was kept at the coal mines for several months, leaving his family to cope alone. He was reunited with his relatives for six years, and then he was forced into joining the Soviet Army. His family knew that if war broke out, there was a fair chance that they would never see his face again.

Trouble was rising in the world. Germany came in to try to protect the Ukrainians from the Communists. The Communists took possession of the Stojcenko family's land and farm. They were given a small portion of land to work on. All their produce was given to the Communists. Schools were closed when Katherina was fifteen. The family could no longer make any money and were starving, despite their desperate efforts. Stalin had also burnt the food supplies of towns nearby. The Ukraine was one of the worst and most frightening countries to be in during the rise of Communism.

Stalin did not want anybody standing in the way of his takeover of Eastern Europe with Communism. The people who were most likely to do this were well educated, wealthy, intuitive and hard-working. People like the Stojcenkos. Along with millions of others, Basil's two brothers and his parents who lived next door were seized and transported by train to Siberia in 1930, three months after my grandmother was born and Lydia was just three years old. 'My grandparents asked the Communists if they could see the babies – us – to say goodbye, but they said no,' Katherina says sadly. The Communists were looking over their shoulders as they wrote their final words to loved ones whilst on the train. Martha and her children never got one letter from them, but they knew the fate of their relatives. They would rest forever in a silent land of ice.

Katherina, her siblings and Martha often wrote to Basil, who was then in Germany. On just another stark cold day, a very important letter arrived. Basil told them to stop immediately whatever they were doing and leave for Germany. It was a matter of life and death because the Nazis were coming for them. He knew. At the exact same time, Stalin and the Communists were coming to kill them. In 1944, thousands left their homeland with just what they were wearing. 'Very bad. We left everything. We had no spoon, knife or pillow – nothing.' They had to leave behind everything they had worked their entire lives for.

For weeks they had been solidly walking, except for Alexander, who was only six years old and had a place on the cart dragged by their horse. Taya had also come with them and had given birth to a beautiful calf. At night, they would seek shelter and some warmth in barns or, if possible, in the houses of farmers, but they could never stay long and did not always have something to eat or drink. They lost their sense of belonging and safety. They came to a wide river, the Dnieper, crowded with people on its banks. Everyone was dumping everything they carried on the ground and clambering onto the large rafts that would take them across. The extra weight from animals and belongings would make them sink, but most of the rafts still toppled over. Animals were struggling helplessly to cross the river and Katherina let Taya try, as she would die from starvation if she did not cross. The Stojcenkos had no choice but to leave everything behind. They quickly boarded the rafts and made it across safely. On the other side, there was a man surrounded by animals that had swum across the river. Katherina hoped with all her heart that her cow would be there. The man said that if the cow would come when her name was called, she could run away with her. Katherina called out 'Taya!' and, amazingly, Taya came running towards her, but without the calf. Nobody knew what happened to the calf – had she been stolen or drowned? It made Taya very distressed, but she was happy to be back with Katherina.

Nearing Poland, they found Basil at a farmhouse and were again a complete family. He had escaped the army not just because he could have been killed fighting, but because Stalin was killing his own men. He risked his own life and his family's. Basil advised Katherina to give Taya to the farmer because she would not survive their journey anymore. Tearfully, Katherina did so and they were given a bag of apples in exchange. After they crossed the border they were fortunate enough to get a train trip which saved them weeks of walking, begging and eating from rubbish tins. The Stojcenkos travelled through countries including Hungary and Yugoslavia before they reached Austria.

In Austria, they were on the brink of starvation and they all worked on farms and railways to receive food. The farmers were as generous as they could be and gave Katherina's family a sense of belonging, despite being far from their home country. Sometimes, they would find a place to stay – usually one tiny room for the whole family. When they reached Germany, they witnessed the true horrors of the war.

The Americans frequently bombarded the German forms of transport and the workers had to cram into any bomb shelter they could find. In the middle of a freezing night there was a bombing raid and Martha and Basil rushed their slumbering children out of bed and into one of the bomb shelters, disguised in the forest by vegetation. They waited with hundreds of others in the dirty, revolting shelter, listening in terror to the planes circling perilously above. Children sat silently, caressed in their parents' arms, with grim looks on their faces. An explosion came, but not on their shelter. The ground shook and rumbled. They left the shelter to encounter a great shock. The commotion of just minutes before had transformed into a solemn silence. The dead littered the streets. Katherina could not absorb what had happened. Everything was still and no one had been spared. There was no movement except for the eerie floating of feathers through the air. Feathers from the quilts that had kept little ones warm before their deaths. 'I felt very sad, very sad because everybody was killed. But I felt happy because my brothers, sister, mother and father were not hurt. Thank God for that.'

The Stojcenkos stayed in an English zone of Germany for a few weeks. They had to beg for food and were prepared to eat mouldy bread just to ease their hunger. Katherina did not shower and wore the same clothes all the time. When they moved into the American zone, Basil organised for them to be transported to Brazil as refugees. The Americans would let them go to any South American country but not Australia or America because a family of six people was not wanted in either. In 1949, the family left Europe. In my grandmother's case, she would never return to Ukraine.

In Brazil, life was better because the country was at peace, but it was not great. Katherina was nineteen and worked in bread and jam factories. She attended the Ukrainian church with her family and met the Selinski family, who had also fled the Ukraine. One of the eight children was Alex, who was twenty years old. Alex and Katherina were soon married and had a baby girl, Nadia, my mother. Three years later they had Tamara. Alex organised passports and ship tickets to Australia to start a new life and to escape some of Brazil's problems. When Katherina was twenty-eight, the Selinskis left Brazil on a ship which went past Spain and France and down the Suez Canal.

Australia was strange and foreign for Katherina. She did not know a word of English and did not have much money. Australia did give her and her family more opportunities. There was more work and better schools and it was much cleaner. At school, Nadia and Tamara were called 'wogs' and Nadia was nicknamed 'Nana-banana.' Their real names were ignored and the pirozhki and borsch they ate were disgusting to their classmates. Katherina's sister-in-law was forced to cover up her front windows with wood during the Cold War because the council suspected them of being Soviet spies.

My grandmother now lives near me. She has three daughters and ten grandchildren. 'I'm glad I came to Australia and I love this country as much as my old country. I am happy my children and grandchildren live here and have grown up here. I hope they will never have to go through what I did,' she says.

We Were Chosen:
Mrs Z's Story

by Iman Zayegh, aged 13

I was sick of it all . . . sick of the cold dreary mornings, the dark gloomy nights and the almost always overcast sky. The nightmares and that vague feeling that you were being followed were always with you wherever you went. It was the effects of the war, effects that are not easily disposed of.

I was born in my hometown, in my native country Lebanon and, up until I was eleven, this is where I lived. It was a wonderful village that I lived in: small and friendly. We all knew each other; we were only about fifteen families altogether. We lived happy lives, as we were raised with all our friends and family, and we thought this was the way everyone lived, families, tribes and just people in general.

We were all grateful for what we had, because we knew that, although there were many people much better off than us, there were also many people much worse off. Little did we know that we were about to lose the little that we did have and that we were about to be come face-to-face with an obstacle we would never forget . . .

We had always known that there was trouble between the Lebanese Imperialists and the Lebanese Socialists. My father told us what was going on all the time, and it's just as well he did.

One day, when my father had come home from a long day of work on the farm, he told us that the clashes between the

Lebanese Imperialist and Lebanese Socialist rebels were getting worse. This news worried us all, because we knew if this got much worse civil war would be declared and that would be the end of our happy lives of peace and prosperity.

Although none of us had ever experienced war before, our grandparents had, and the stories they told us about it were enough let us know it wasn't in the least bit an easy thing.

The day we heard the war was declared was the first day of our harvesting season. Little did we know that there would be no work to be done at all. Early that morning as we sat around the breakfast table listening to the radio, we heard an urgent announcement that war had been officially declared due to further clashes between the Lebanese Socialists and Lebanese Imperialists.

We were told that the living conditions might gradually worsen and some of life's essentials such as electricity and water might be rationed; and that all citizens were to stay indoors at all times. We knew that, having a huge family with no power, water or access to outside life, we would be ruined and could not survive.

When we heard that chances of immigration to a foreign country were provided for a limited number of families, my dad volunteered without hesitation. He knew that it would be hard for us to cope and move to another country and he knew that the chances of being chosen to immigrate out of all the other families would be slim; nevertheless, he thought that anything would be better than living in a war-torn country.

We registered along with the other families that wanted to immigrate and because we were one of the first to do so I thought we had a pretty good chance. In fact I was almost certain that we would be chosen. I was excited by the idea but also very, very nervous and afraid of what would happen on the way out of the country and at the borders. I was getting used to hearing the sounds of bombs going off and gunshots in the distance but when we were travelling towards the gunshots and explosions I was not so sure how safe we would be.

The reply we got from the government shocked us all but most of all me. My dad came home one day as usual and it didn't seem as though anything had happened. In the middle of us having dinner – what I thought would be one of our last – my father calmly said: 'By the way, did I tell you that I got the response from the government and that the families to immigrate are already chosen?'

We all burst into bouts of happiness and joy as we celebrated the fact that we were going to immigrate and get away from the war. We didn't even hear the rest of what father said. Suddenly in an angry tone that he hardly ever used, my father silenced us and explained that we had not been one of the few lucky families to be chosen and that we were not going anywhere. He told us that our reaction was very disappointing because he thought we were proud of our country and our identity. We sat quietly for quite a while thinking and trying to contemplate what was happening, not knowing what to do.

How could this have happened? I wondered. I was almost certain that we were going to be chosen. My father was one of the best farmers in the whole city and I was sure that would win us a place. Obviously I was wrong.

Our life went on as normal for a further two weeks and during that time, we found out that my best friend's family were chosen as one of the families to immigrate and they were leaving very soon. I cried and cried as I bade her farewell and wished her a happy life.

Soon I was over it all, and, although the war was still raging as fierce as ever I got used to it and adapted. I understood the fact that we weren't chosen and accepted it, knowing that there were people who needed this chance more than we did. Just as I started to feel a little glad we were still at home something happened, something no one was expecting, something that changed my life and my whole family's life forever.

One evening, an evening when the fighting was particularly bad, as I was working on a new piece of embroidery I had started, my father ran into the house after arriving early from work. 'We made it! We made it!' he yelled. 'We were chosen, yes we were! Another family pulled out last minute and we were next in line!' He seemed so happy, happier than I'd ever seen him before and as soon as I heard the news I was so overwhelmed with happiness that I didn't know what to say or do. Instead I started crying. I didn't mean to, I mean I didn't even know I would, but I did.

Suddenly my whole family stopped their celebrations and came and sat around me. They tried to comfort me and reassure me that I would make new friends in our new home. They told me that they would miss the country too but we would soon have a new home to share and a new life to live away from danger.

At that point I stopped. I'd given them the wrong impression; they thought I didn't want to go, but it was actually on the contrary. I was ecstatic about the trip and I told them that. As I returned to my room in a state of disbelief, I wondered to myself why I had cried. As I sat down on my bed, suddenly I realised: it was because I was overjoyed. They were tears of joy but it wasn't that simple. They were also tears that were brought about by fear and confusion, fear that my dream, this fantasy I was about to live would come to an end, that all the happiness and joy would go to waste and that our plans would all be destroyed. That my dream life would remain a dream forever and never become reality. I was afraid of all that, afraid about the journey, the arrival and the struggle to survive in a foreign land.

Finally the time came to leave. After hours and hours of packing and getting ready, checking and double checking we had everything, remembering last-minute things and running off to do them, we were all in a rush between calling friends and saying our last goodbyes. Friends and neighbours who had grown to be part of your life and family now had to be left behind and become merely memories of the past. It was very sad and emotional but I had been prepared. I shed my fair share of tears and with our last goodbyes we climbed into the bus and took our last glance at what was our home for so many years as we drove off into the distance.

The trip through town took five agonising hours, watching, waiting, praying for something good to happen, hoping with all your heart they would let you pass without any problems. Finally, when we did get past, it felt great to know we were on free land that posed no threat to anyone.

I woke up and saw myself in a huge room full of people; they were all passing by quickly on their way to different places, looking very busy. As I turned around I saw the rest of my family sitting next to me waiting anxiously for something to happen. It was then that I realised I didn't know where we were and more importantly I didn't know where we were going. Through all my joy and excitement I had forgotten to ask what country we were immigrating to, and I couldn't wait to find out.

When I asked my father where we were going, I was surprised by his answer but at the same time was glad that I wasn't the last one to know. He said that we were waiting to be told where we were going so we could continue our trip. I also found out that we were in Beirut airport. I was amazed that there was such a great airport in my own city and I had never known about it!

In the end we were told we were to go to Australia. Australia – what a cool name for a country! When we heard the man tell us, at first we didn't really react. All my dad said was thank you and we walked away from the counter. The reason we did not react was because we had never heard of Australia before. I used to think that Lebanon was the only country in the world, but I was wrong. I didn't know about the outside world and quite frankly, I didn't care because I didn't think there would be any need to know: as long as I was in my country with my people that was all that mattered.

It took eight long hours in the aeroplane to Australia and my siblings and I slept most of the way.

We reached Australia and were given a home to live in. We started school and became fluent with the English language. I made new friends and met new people and I was amazed by how friendly everyone was and how they treated each other so well. The beauty of the city we stayed in, Melbourne, also amazed me and although Australia may not be my country I still call it home.

As a Boy:
Aziz Asghar's Story

by Caitlin Gardiner, aged 15

Born: Afghanistan
Age: fifteen
Gender: male
Education: little
Religion: minority
Taliban: legal for them to kill us

They were taking lots of people, back then. Guns were familiar to us and so our skills were valuable for use in the army. They came for my eldest brother. He went and hid in the mountains and when the people came for him, he wasn't there. They wanted the next eldest – me. My father paid them money. He bribed them to keep me safe. But he knew he couldn't hold them off for long. They were going to come back for either money or me, and one day we'd run out of money.

My father woke me in the middle of the night. He told me he was sending me away with my uncle. I didn't know where we were going, but I didn't question them. Respecting and obeying our elders is something deeply ingrained in our culture. Without even a goodbye to the rest of my family, I was hidden in the back of a wood truck and we fled.

People complain that plane trips or long car rides are uncomfortable, but they have never travelled in the back of a wood truck for three days, their legs and back cramping from the tiny space, dust and wood shavings filling their mouth, the uncomfortable jolting of the truck over rocky dirt roads making it impossible to occupy your mind and forget about your situation for even a moment.

For three days I travelled like this across sparsely inhabited country between Afghanistan and Pakistan, holed up in the back of the truck like a sheep or cow being transported to the abattoirs. I first realised we had reached the border into Pakistan when I heard the rough voice of a Pakistani border official asking for my uncle and the driver's IDs. I hadn't begun to feel nervous until this moment – my mind had been occupied with unanswerable questions about where I was headed – but now my heart was pounding. I felt that adrenaline-induced nervousness fluttering in my stomach every time I took a breath. What if he turned the truck back into Afghanistan? What if he decided to search the truck? I waited for one tortured moment, motionless amongst the wood, afraid to breathe for fear of making a sound. The official glanced at the documents, decided everything was in order, and let us go. I peered through the gaps in the wood at the back of the truck, watching as the border officers got smaller and smaller, further and further away from me.

The week in Pakistan passed in a confusion-fuelled blur. Before I knew it I was sitting on a plane to Indonesia.

But Indonesia was not to be my final destination. Here, in Indonesia, I learnt that the country we were headed for, the country that would offer me safety and freedom and unimaginable opportunities, was the magical and mysterious land of Australia.

The boat I came over on was one of the last boats to take refugees from Indonesia to Australia. I arrived in Australia in August 2001, a month before September 11, and before Australia tightened national security in the aftermath of the Bali bombings. The boat was small and crowded and reeked of dead fish and dried salt. The splintery wooden deck creaked with the strain of many years as people stepped aboard. What was meant to be a small fishing vessel had over 350 people cramped together on board. A man dispensed some advice before I boarded: 'You just have to run and find a place on the boat for yourself, don't worry about anyone else, otherwise you'll get left behind.' Heeding his warning, I ran fast, with my small satchel on my back, thinking only of myself, my safety, my freedom.

The first two days the weather was clear, the water blue and sparkling. I sat on the deck and talked to another refugee from Afghanistan, relaxing in the sun. A growing feeling of hope was emerging inside me for the first time since I had left home.

On the second day, the birds began circling and the warm breeze turned into an icy gale. A storm was approaching. The water became black and stormy, and the waves were higher than I have ever seen. A murmur of panic ran through the crowd. The terrifyingly high waves towered over us and the furious ocean tossed the tiny boat around like a toy. Thunder broke and the rain began to pour down. I shivered in my thin shirt as I crouched next to my friend, both of us praying for safety, for God to save us. We thought death was certain. Any moment we would be swamped by a crashing wave and swept under. Our fear was heightened by the fact that none of us could swim. We would be swallowed up in the swirling depths with no hope of survival. I began to weep. My friend put his arm around me. 'Listen,' he said. 'You have two options – to be alive or to die. If God wants you to die, you will die, but if not, you won't, so don't fret.' His words comforted me. They gave me hope that God would get me through this, and if not, he had a good reason for me to die.

After a night of misery, the next morning dawned bright and clear, with the kind of fresh, clean feeling present after a storm. Although we were thankful that we were alive, we were still reliving the terror of the night before and the day was spent in a mournful, dulled state of mind. We had just about given up hope. Somebody had discovered a hole in the boat; not big enough to cause trouble, but still another problem to add to our growing list of concerns. We thought we were destined to starve or drown at sea, never to be heard of again. That night I sat on the roof with my friend, watching the waves. Gently they rocked me into a peaceful state. It was late, the night was quiet and still. After a while, I noticed in the distance a light, a distant, twinkling beam. At first it didn't register as anything important. To me it looked like any one of the stars in the sky, so visible out on the ocean. But gradually it grew bigger and bigger, and I realised it wasn't in the sky – it was on land. I jumped up, ran in circles, screaming in jubilation that we were saved. The other passengers woke, grumbling that I had disturbed them, but then they saw it too and a bright spark of hope flashed across their faces. We were crazy with happiness . . . yelling, hugging, dancing. As we neared land we saw roads and cars. We lit fires to signal the people ashore, but it was as if nobody saw us, nobody cared. A police boat appeared, zipping across the waves, proclaiming that this was Christmas Island, and we weren't welcome. All the misery of the past few weeks compounded in that one moment of despair. We desperately begged to be allowed to stay. We had come so far, prayed, suffered, hoped and despaired, and it had all come to nothing. But they were indifferent to our pleas. 'Sorry, there's nothing we can do,' they told us. 'It's not up to us. We just can't let you in.' Then one man jumped up. 'There's a hole in the boat,' he yelled, his voice on the point of hysteria. 'If you turn us away we'll sink.' Looks of hesitation crossed their faces. A refugee boat full of holes is turned away from Australia by officials who knew it was likely to sink. Doesn't look too good in the papers, does it? Finally, it was decided. We were allowed to enter Christmas Island but from here we would be sent directly to Port Hedland detention centre.

If I had have known the unbelievable anguish I would suffer there, I think I would have taken my chances on the leaky boat.

We drove up to the gate. I saw the wire, the fence, the dust, the small portables. Surely this wasn't Australia? A thousand thoughts were hammering in my head – I was like a tantrum-throwing child. Why do they lock us up? This shouldn't happen to children. If I were Australian would it be different? Did anyone care that I was alone, in a foreign country where I didn't speak the language? Didn't anyone care that I had run from death? Why was I being locked up?

Never-ending. Endless. Continual. Non-stop. Eternal. Infinite. Incessant. Everlasting. How many words are there for the never-ending? Locked up. Days of nothing. Time endless, imprisoned in desolation.

I am trapped in this place I call home.

They say, *Go away. Go home, illegal queue jumper.*

I say, *Let me stay. They'll kill me; they'll take me away, and make me fight for them.*

I feel like no one wants to know me.

Does anybody care I know no one?

I have no friends.

I have no one. Hostility is following me and stalking me with fearful stares. Fear because I am different. I don't conform to their belief of what is normality. A normal life. *Why don't they come the proper way? On planes, through immigration?* I am a prisoner who has committed no crime. What was my offence punishable by law? Obeying my father? Running from pain, death, hurt? This is a jail. A prison. A detention centre. They keep us locked up, to keep the country secure, to keep you safe from the invaders. *Please let me out. Please*, we beg. Children cry. Hunger, protests, suicide swarm around us like angry bees. Thoughts swirling in my head, never leaving me alone.

Help me. I'm sinking.

Deeper and deeper. Life is futile. Go away. Let me go away.

I don't want to live in this oppressive, depressive captivity. I can't stand this barrage of thoughts, this harmful, relentless beast in my head.

But then it came . . .

A letter.

It came in the mail like a lifeline thrown off the side of a boat. It was a simple letter; an introduction, telling me about herself, her situation, her family, but to me it was like the first delicious bite of an apple after weeks of starvation. It was a rope pulling me up. I was sinking. I didn't want to come back up, but it wrapped itself around me and held on, jerked me up. More letters came, heaving me slowly out of the dark into the light. They called and I answered. I came back. They gave me a sense of freedom that I hadn't enjoyed in a long time. I could let out all my pain and uncertainty. I had a friend. Physically, I was still imprisoned, but emotionally I had my freedom. Freedom from pain and suffering, from depression and loneliness. I had been hoping for release; a release from the emotional pain of the detention centres and from the jail itself. I had one of these. It was only a matter of time before I got both.

Name: Aziz
Living: Australia
Age: eighteen
Religion: none
Education: starting Year Twelve
Taliban: a memory
Current situation: released from detention – awaiting court
   decision on future.

The Wheat Fields: Michael Booker's Story

by Nicholas James Cooper, aged 19

I sit in this crop circle of mine in the middle of the swaying river. I hear my father calling me even though he knows where I am. He can see how the small flattened area is causing the stalks behind it to be pushed further by the wind, making a shape like Halley's Comet and lighting up my presence. He knows the wheat fields a lot better then I do.

I can see him now, letting his hand hover over the ears of wheat, a roughened, fingered stump against the golden slender plants. I can feel his pride in his creations, which have grown tall, healthy and survived the drought.

He can see me but cannot feel my pain; he has never been anywhere near where I have to go. I feel trapped and cornered like one of our dogs was when the dingoes came down from the hills looking for streams and pools of water in the drought. They came to the dam and the kelpie tried to push them off. They were desperate to have what they wanted and they entered into a stand-off; they wanted different things and one of them had to give in.

I don't want to leave and get a ride to the city in my brother's rig tonight. I want to wait and celebrate.

As long as I can remember it has felt weird cutting down what we spend nine and a half months growing but my father always enjoys it. These fields will look so bare with only the wheat's grey stubble left, yet there will be the good soil, the potential that matters. But we both know that it will have potential just like it had last year and that out of it will grow a new crop and a new income.

We always have a special meal after harvest; the wheat will have been bundled into sectors ready to catch a ride to the silos. I'll be preparing for another summer of lazing in the grain, waiting only for the next truck to come in, the next seed to be packed or to be planted. We invite everyone who has helped throughout the year yet it always ends up including everyone who did not. Throughout the night people discuss farming matters and town meetings take place. No one goes to church the next morning. We eat in the barn. Everyone brings something that they are known for, be it food, drink or a violin. And so the whole community drinks merrily and dances naturally, while ribs crackle and sausages sizzle on the hot tray. It is a day for the older generation (as I am made to say) to leave the RSL and to come and nostalgically remember the past, chanting 'remember this and remember that.' Mother says we have been doing this here for over sixty years, and while wiping my hands on her apron, I secretly wish that maybe, when I am old, I will be able to do the same. The barn's beams creak but stay strong, just like us.

My father will be in the corner digging into the cans, but he'll deserve it: this year's crop will be a ripper. He'll get the new machinery and irrigation he wants. Next year there won't be enough work for him, let alone someone else. 'Just follow suit,' he says, 'you'll be right.' Well, my brother left to be a truckie, and my sister is long gone, married, to some place near Brisbane, living in a high-rise apartment with aircon and delivery pizza.

Lawyers and doctors don't have a harvest to celebrate: the seasons stopped when they graduated, to be locked into a spell, only to be unbroken when retirement nears. They don't need to know the river and dam connections, only the timetable of the subway. No need for 'roo tracks or fence-lines; only for traffic lights, walls and freeways. No need for your body; only for your brain.

My father gets fed up with waiting and retreats inside. But I wait there rocking, knees drawn up, listening to my breath that is in union with the field's: hoarse and guttural, knowing the end is near. Once it is nearly dark, my brother is sent out to find me. He doesn't know the fields and gets lost. I hear him swishing around cursing everything while calling out my name. He ends up returning to the family, empty handed, similar to the prodigal son out of the Bible, but father doesn't welcome him as kindly and me neither when he wrenches me inside. He believes what he is doing is right and that between my finger and thumb a squat pen should rest: as snug as a gun, confused.

He never really thought about it and that summer he had to all at once. He spoke to my mother and people from the city but he didn't speak to me.

I got in the truck with my bags as he wished, said a few good-byes and told them they were doing the wrong thing, the land was where I belonged not the great family tradition of boarding school. They told me to trust them, to 'give it a go.'

We pull in at Saundra Service Station. Chris climbs down to refuel and check the ribbed tires, leaving me in the capacious cabin. I don't want to go to the city to learn to be someone I don't want to be, to do a job I don't want to do. I don't want to leave home but I know that I cannot return, so I decide to climb down as well. I take my bag and set off somewhere to make my own home. Off into the darkness, to find an in-between . . .

~

It is hot as I drive back out to my parents; the whining from the back gets louder as the journey lengthens. My family seems to think that it is more fun having Christmas at home and I seem to be the only one who does not get bored with the landscape; but, then again, I know the wheat fields a lot better then they do.

We are Now in This One Place

by Deng Elia, Kuach Deng and Atem Jok, aged 16

We are three boys from Sudan, Kuai, Haji and Kuet. In Sudan, we didn't know each other, but if we just meet, we would call each other Sudan dudes. We were all in Panyuduk and Kakuma, but we didn't meet. We didn't know each other before. Now we are together in this place in Australia.

This is Kuai's story

My name is Kuai. I don't know exactly how old I am, but I think I am sixteen. I was born in my mother's tribe's place, in a small town called Panyuduk. We lived there for a long time. Then one day, my dad came and picked us up and took us to Kaaya. I was about four years old.

We lived with my sister and her husband and my brothers and sisters. In that day, everyone wanted to live. We were under attack. I went away with my mother and father, and one brother and two sisters. We went to Bhar el Ghazal. My other brothers remained. I don't know where they went.

We lived in Bhar el Ghazal for one year. After that, my sister, the second born, went to live in Bor. Then my dad was caught by the soldiers. They wanted him to go and fight for them. I was living with my mum and my brother and sister in Gogrial. My mum was looking for her husband, and was always walking around the town. There was a war on in Gogrial, and people were fighting each other. It was a dangerous place.

My sister got married in Gogrial and she went to live in Khartoum with her husband. I spent one year in Gogrial with my mum and my brother, and then we moved to Wau. We saw my father and we spent about four months there. Then we went to Khartoum in a train, a big tall one.

After we went, my father was killed. He was driving along the road and he passed over a mine. My uncle found him. My father said to him, 'Go and tell my wife and children.' He was talking but he wanted to die. My uncle went to Khartoum, but he didn't want to tell us, but another person came and told us. My mother cried, and us, too.

My sister and her husband lived alone in Khartoum. But they were fighting every day. My mum went there and took her away. We went to a corner in Khartoum for the Sudanese. Arabs and Sudanese lived together in that city, and there was a place for each one. We lived there maybe two or three years. Then we went back to Bhar el Ghazal.

We stayed there about a year. Then the husband of my older sister gave us a refugee card from the UN. We went by car to Lokichoggia and then to the Kakuma refugee camp in Kenya. We stayed there about one month. My mum went back to Sudan. My older sister sent someone to get me and I went to live with her in Nairobi, just me alone. After a year my brother came to visit us. He stayed one month and then he went back to Kakuma.

One day someone said there was a headcount so we all went back to Kakuma. After one month we came back to Nairobi. Then they repeated the headcount because some people didn't get cards, so we went back again.

One day we met a cousin, and he gave us a form to go to Australia. He comes from the same tribe, and he is one of the lost boys from Sudan. Now he is in Australia, but he was there then. My sister filled in the form, and my uncle paid all the money for us. He paid the money for the medical and the interview and the fare to fly here to Australia.

There were eight of us. We all came to Australia on 2nd January 2004. There was my older sister and her four children, my sister who is seventeen, and my uncle's little girl, who is about three, and me. My sister's husband is still in Kenya and my mother is somewhere in Sudan. One day, we hope they can come here, too.

This is Haji's story

My name is Haji. I am sixteen years old. I'm Sudanese by nationality. I was born in Sudan in Bor, in a small village called Marol. We lived in the part called Lualajokbil. In 1990, our village was being attacked by gunmen in the military, so we moved from our village to Madiing. We came from there with my father. He was a soldier. He took us to Madiing, and came back to the village to fight.

In 1991 he had been killed, and the government military kept moving until they came to Madiing. On one night, they attacked the people there, and my mother ran away with my little brother and my little sister. I escaped with my eldest sister and we went into the bush. We met my cousin's daughter and her brother and we travelled together.

We walked until we came to the Ethiopian border. We were taken by the leaders to join the camp in Ethiopia, a place called Pochala for children without parents. After a while, we moved to Panyuduk for around three months. From Panyuduk we crossed a river called Gilo to go to Buma. There were a lot of people missing, because the river was flowing very hard. It's a sad story, eh?

We kept moving from Buma to Narus and then we went to Lokichoggia in Kenya. We went on, and on. Then, on 28th February 1992, we arrived in Kakuma refugee camp. My cousin's son went to live with the minors, a group of boys who had lost their parents. I stayed together with my sister and my cousin's daughter. The situation was going good for us. We could go to school, and we had medicine.

In 2001, I found one of my mothers, the other wife of my father. She was in Kakuma. She listened to the people talk and looked for me, and she found me there. She is still there, in Kakuma. I lost my real mum, and I don't know where she is.

In 2001, my cousin's son went to the United States, so we remained three, I and my sister, and my cousin's daughter. In 2002, the husband to the sister of my uncle sent us a form for resettlement to Australia. He is here now in this place, but he was in Kakuma before. My cousin's son paid the money for us to come. In 2004, on 8th March, we travelled to Australia, we three.

This is Kuet's story

Hello, this is Kuet. I am sixteen. I am Sudanese, and my tribe is from Bor. I was born in Ethiopia, and I stayed there with my mum and my brother for about five years. We stayed with my uncle and his wife. My uncle was a captain, a soldier. He was also a doctor. In that day, there were people in Ethiopia who used to bully and kill Sudanese people. They had a different language. My dad and a brother were in a place called Panyuduk. My mum and I and my older brother, and my uncle and his wife went in a car to Addis Ababa. From there we went to Gambella. Then we came to Panyuduk. I was six years old.

At Panyuduk we used to run after the big trucks and grab hold of them, and climb up on top. The trucks were carrying wheat flour, called papa. We used to eat it, and it was very sweet. The trucks had trailers behind them, just like a road train. The road was down in the river. The river was dry, and the trucks travelled along it. We used to play football there too.

One day we were playing there and three big trucks came. One boy kicked the ball at the side of the river. I ran across, but the trucks came and knocked me down. I fell to the ground and they ran over me. I lay down very straight and the wheels went both sides of me. It happened one morning and I wasn't hurt, but it shocked and winded me.

One of my brothers was really good at climbing on the trucks. He would climb up and throw the wheat flour down to us. One day we saw a man fall from a truck. He was on the truck with us. He tried to jump from one trailer to another. He fell down and the wheels ran right over his head and he was killed. We were hanging on the back and we saw it happen. When we saw that, we stopped going on the trucks. It was too dangerous.

We stayed some time in Pochala and then we moved to Lokichoggia. We came to Kenya when I was six years old. It was Christmas time, 1994. We went to Kabes and stayed there about a year. We used to eat bananas and go fishing. From there we went to Narus, and then back to Lokichoggia. Then we went to Kakuma and to the camp. It was around 1995 to 1996.

Kakuma was a dangerous place. It was cold and there were windstorms. There were always windy problems. Sometimes it was like fog with dirt in it. I went to preschool in Kakuma. I was eight years old. I had two friends, and we all went to preschool together.

In 1998, I went back to Narus to stay with my mother. I stayed three months and then I went back to Kakuma. I was supposed to go to school, but I played every day. I would leave home in the morning, and I would stay away all day. I talked with people, and danced, and I played pool. I was nine years old. We never went to school, just to preschool. Our books were blank and no writing in them at all. My friend's mum asked us, 'What are they doing at school?' but we didn't know.

I was staying with my dad, but I was always together with my friends. We knew every corner in Kakuma. We were good dancers. We used to dance and everyone used to come and watch us. We played football with the other boys down in the dry river bed. There is one boy here now in this place and I knew him from before. He used to play football with us then.

In 1999, my dad began the process with the UN to go to another country. First we were going to America, but the forms broke up. We tried in 2000, 2001 and 2002 but the forms broke up. Then in 2003 we got the forms for Australia. We went for an interview and a medical, and then we came to Australia.

I am glad to be here. It is good because there is no fighting now. Kakuma was a dangerous place. I'm happy now. If I was still in Kakuma, I would have no chance. I thank God I am here in Australia. If you find another Sudanese boy, everything is good. We boys are happy. We know that a few things happen still. People can annoy you, but things happen the same everywhere.

I came here first, in 2003, on 25th February. I said, 'I just know that some of my friends will come,' so I waited. Kuai came first and I met him, and now I know him. Then Haji came. We didn't know him before. Haji came and met us, so now we know him. We are doing maths together, and English. Haji told us the type he is, and where he was living in Sudan. We didn't know each other before that day.

I've been here one year, and Kuai for six months and Haji for three. Now we are in this place together. It is a time for learning and to get more education. Most boys here are learning. If we will go back to Africa, then Africa will be a good place. I will come with the things I know, and Haji and Kuai, and all the boys will come with what they know, and life will be good in Sudan. It will be better.

In ten years, perhaps I will be back in Africa, but if I had my mum here, there is no need to go back. You can't stop thinking of your parents. You can only be happy if you know where they are, your brothers and sisters and parents, and if they can be with you. If my mum and brothers and cousins can be here with me, I'd be a citizen for real. If your mum is here, you'll be free. That is what we want the most.

SOMETHING ABOUT LOVE

'Doing what I do for my people makes me proud.
I am noticed. Not just a shadow anymore. I have
found my face and I know where it's looking.'

Carla Johnson

My Hope – Lili and Elek Gelbart's Journey to Australia

by Sarah Gelbart, aged 16

15th April 1945: some people would describe it as the end. Now it seems more like a turning point on the way to a new life. I can't see myself there anymore. It is just incomprehensible to me that we survived. Now, sitting here in the comforts of my Melbourne home, surrounded by a wonderful family, I think: why go back? Back to that country, back to the pain, back to the hunger, back to the violence and hatred? Then I think of my grandchildren, proud, free Australians. I think of all we have worked for. And I come to the conclusion that they should know, so that future generations can learn from the mistakes of history. However, I physically can't do it. I can't open up those wounds, those wounds that never heal. No matter how much care they are given, those wounds leave an inerasable scar. As Jozef Zelkowicz of Lodz Ghetto said, 'Listen and believe this, even though it happened then, even though it seems so old, so distant and so strange.' It will take every ounce of your imagination, but try . . .

15th April 1945: the day you are liberated by the British from Bergen Belsen Concentration Camp. You look like a walking skeleton. At twenty-five years of age, you weigh just thirty-five kilograms, and are a mere shadow of your former self. You are surrounded by starvation and disease, death stares you in the face. You have been in this hell-on-Earth for just over a week, without a scrap of food or a drop of water. For the past nine excruciating months, you have been transported from Auschwitz to Falkenberg, to Bergen Belsen, to Hildersheim and finally back to Bergen Belsen. As if that is not enough, from the beginning of 1940 until its liquidation in August 1944, you were contained in the Lodz Ghetto. There you worked under slave-labour conditions for the German war effort. After nearly six years incarcerated behind bars for the simple crime of being born Jewish, you are given a new lease on life.

This seems like a lot to take in, however it gets worse. Upon searching, you discover that *none* of your family survived. Not your parents, not your brother, grandparents, cousins, aunts, uncles. You are completely alone in the world. Where do you begin? How does one go about building a new life? In Bergen Belsen you meet your wife-to-be. She too was in Lodz, Auschwitz and numerous other concentration and labour camps. She understands what you have been through, and together you decide to make a new start.

Where should you go? Staying in Germany is not an option, with all that has gone on here. And Poland, your birthplace, is now occupied by the Soviet Union. You need to free yourself from the memories of these places. Together you consult a map of the world. Australia looks good. Its unique geographical location puts it about as far away as humanly possible from Europe (man hasn't landed on the moon yet). It appears to be as far away from the anti-Semitic nightmare you have been living for the past six years and prior. Far away from those haunting images of your family and your people burning in the crematorium of Auschwitz-Birkenau.

You have heard good reports of Australia, and know they are accepting displaced persons from Europe. Your wife has some family in Melbourne who left Poland before the war. With the help of the Red Cross you are able to apply for an entry permit. This all seems simple enough. However there could be a problem.

There is a quota for the number of Jews allowed to enter Australia. Your wife's sister and brother also survived the war and are looking to come out to Australia too. As Jews from Europe, you are an unknown, with a different heritage, different culture and beliefs. How would you cope in Australia? How will you fit in?

Your first son is born on 10th February 1947. It is a very proud moment for you, after all that has happened. You are still in Germany, waiting for a boat to Australia. After six months, you are told it would be quicker if you go via France. In France information arrives that in two weeks a ship is coming that will take you to your new home. However the ship does not arrive. In the meantime, you are given a subsidy to be put up in a rundown hotel in Paris. You stay in a tiny room on the third floor, with hardly enough room for a bed, a small table and two chairs. You cook off a miniature gas camping stove, which is a serious fire hazard. During your stay, you go on a day outing to the famous Père Lachaise Cemetery, and are overwhelmed by the beauty of the gardens and immaculate state of the graves dating back to the 1400s. It provides a powerful juxtaposition with the mass graves you left behind in Germany and evokes harrowing memories. News comes that your ship to Australia is here. After seven months, you finally depart France, depart Europe, and leave your past behind. As you pull out of the Port of Marseilles, you don't look behind you, but rather turn your back on the past and focus on the present and the future. On this ship, the *Misr*, you place all your aspirations. Full steam ahead to a new and better life in Australia.

The journey is five weeks long. It was planned to take four, however, the ship has a problem, and you spend a week docked in Colombo. On board you are separated from your wife and son, as women and children sleep four to a cabin in First Class. The *Misr* is a seven-thousand tonne boat that was built during the war to transport soldiers to the various battlefields. You are supposed to sleep below deck, but on the first night you go down and see it is overcrowded and cramped. You take a blanket and sleep in a corner on the deck. It is quite hot, and sleeping under the stars is revitalising. You feel free and alive. However the journey is not so pleasurable for all. The majority of the passengers on board become badly seasick. It is strange going to the dining hall for breakfast, and being the only person there, when two or three hundred people are scheduled to eat. You have countless waiters there to serve you.

The voyage has become a liberating experience. Being outside, with the fresh sea breeze and the majestic azure water that stretches to the horizon and beyond, has done you the world of good. It is now 28th April 1948, a beautiful autumn day. With a clear blue sky and the sun shining brightly, you see land up ahead that looks green and inviting. As you pull into Port Phillip Bay, the ship slows right down. It is as if everything is in slow motion. Standing on deck, taking it all in, your eyes are affixed on this land. This is your future. What can you expect? What will it be like? You dock at Melbourne's Station Pier. Enter the chance at a new life.

～

Sometimes I feel as though my past is a story that happened to someone else. Yet the memories are engraved forever in my mind. No matter how much I try to block them out, they will always be a part of me. This is not necessarily such a bad thing, for it was those events and memories that have made me who I am today. Those memories have made me a more resilient and stronger person. Though sometimes I still can't believe it was me who survived. My wife, my son and I made it here and were able to begin a new life here in Australia. We are eternally grateful to the Australian people and government for accepting us. In my wildest fantasies back in Europe, I could not have dreamt that my life would end up like this.

Still, it was not easy when we first arrived. Imagine not

knowing a single word of English, trying to find work, support a family and adjust to a completely new culture and way of life.

I remember walking down the street with a few strange coins in my hand . . . remember walking into the bakery and pointing to something that was unfamiliar but looked interesting. Then I held out my hand with the coins, as the shop assistant took my money. We had to trust everybody. When you consider where we had just come from, where everyone and everything was against us, that was not so easy! However the Australian people were all extremely kind and welcoming. Everyone we met was helpful and tried to make our transition into this new country a positive experience.

After we arrived here, we met up with my wife's brother and sister who had also survived the war. Their families came out shortly after us. This was an incredibly emotional time. They were our only connection to our past, to Europe. Together our three families moved into a house in Glen Iris. There were nine of us in total, with three children under the age of two. It was a cosy home, and whilst we men went out to work, our wives stayed at home and looked after the children.

We listened to the radio, examined newspapers and whatever material we could get hold of, and so we began to learn English. I attended one basic English class, but the instructor said that I knew too much already, and there was little point in staying. After the war there was no unemployment and the economy flourished. I managed to find a job at General Motors. In the beginning I was just assembling parts. However, I was curious and showed particular interest in my work. I wanted to understand how the cars were put together. Work regulations were fairly lax, and many people slacked off. However I spent my break time learning how things worked. I was soon promoted and worked my way up through the company to a respectable job and a wage that allowed me to support my family. I enjoyed my time there and was rewarded for my dedication.

In 1954, shortly after the birth of my second son, I officially became an Australian citizen. I remember the interview, having to explain my background, and swearing allegiance to the Queen. This was a natural step for me. It was something that as soon as I got here, I felt was important. I wanted to be accepted as an Australian. I now have no ties with Poland, aside from a handful of childhood memories. My loyalty lies with Australia, and I have absolutely no regrets in coming here.

Like most refugees, when we came to Australia we had nothing. Through a strong work ethic, determination and courage we were able to get to where we are today. My wife and I are now happily retired. I have two children and five grandchildren. They are proud Australians and are aware of their background. I love this country, the people and the way of life. It is the rich multi-cultural society that makes Australia such a wonderful place. People of all different colours, creeds and backgrounds have united to make this country what it is today. My hope is that this will always be the case.

Crimson Sky

by Christine Chung, aged 17

Sometimes I felt as though it happened to someone else, that I was just watching from another pair of eyes. It took me quite a while to grasp the fact that it was actually *real* and that it *did* happen to me. I remember often thinking – no, hoping – that it was just a dream from which I had yet to awaken. This is my story of when I escaped the bloodbath in Dili, East Timor.

It was some time in July 1999 – I remember because I was just starting my second year in high school with the rest of my friends, oblivious to the future that was coming our way. We thought it was just another rebellious action, one of the things that the authorities could handle easily. But it wasn't. Not one of us could ever have predicted the events that were about to unfold.

At first it was people protesting in a central location and then over time it turned into a mass gathering that would sometimes block the main streets for hours. The tension increased each day with the older folks talking in whispers and then the town gossips spreading rumours about the native militia taking over this capital city, and quite possibly the province, from the clutches of the Republic of Indonesia.

I heard talk about politics and war every day from people who came to visit my family, even from the servants. They talked in hushed and conspiratorial voices, as if they were afraid that others might hear what they said and take them away, never to return. I remember thinking that they'd gone mad!

As days passed and it was becoming a risk just to go outside the house, I couldn't contain my anxiety any longer and I asked my dad about the safety of our family. His answer was simple: 'Don't worry, God is always looking out for us. Just you wait, in a couple of days everything will be back to normal.' The way he said it – as if he would bet his life on it – made my worries disappear. But I should have been prepared when I started seeing hatred and violence taking over the personalities of people I once thought I knew – after all, most people are not at their best during times of trouble.

Then one afternoon while I was all alone, the reality hit me. And it hit me hard. One thought kept repeating itself in my head, *we might not survive this*. I remember feeling this dreadful sensation in my heart, one that made it hurt even when I breathed. And after this revelation, instead of feeling miserable about life itself, I felt the anger build up inside me. I had no idea what I was angry about or with whom. But at that time, I was overcome by rage – a fiery anger that made me bite my lip so hard it nearly bled. I wanted to yell at the world for letting this happen in the first place, cry out against the casualties, and tear open the earth with my bare hands so that it would swallow up everything bad that existed. I was so angry, yet I did nothing except lie awake silently on my bed.

As August was approaching, the sound of gunfire became a constant occurrence; at around dinnertime we would expect to hear shots being fired and the other side returning the favour. We heard news about friends who had their houses burned, ran away to live in the mountains to save themselves, and some who died. Houses were attacked by dozens of civilians at once and set fire to after things were taken; the stores lining the busiest street in town were raided by hundreds and left as ruins; and innocent people on the streets were ambushed and beaten to death. A group of militia were feared but it was nothing compared to militia with guns in their hands.

One day, after living with uncertainty for months, my parents told me of the good news, or so it seemed at first. There were a couple of army planes that were willing to transport passengers to a safe place in Indonesia. Initially, I thanked God that finally there was a way out of the nightmare but when I asked Mum where we were all going to stay, I saw her eyes fill with tears and I realised that something was not right. Then in a cracked voice she told me the horrible news – it would only be my brother and me leaving. It took a while for this information to be processed in my mind and then it clicked, they were about to send us out of this hellhole and remain there themselves. As I fought against the onslaught of tears, I packed my bag and lay awake in my bed the whole night wishing with all my might that morning would never come.

It was the most difficult thing I had ever done in my entire life – walking away, unsure of whether I would ever see my dad's good-natured smile, my younger brother's mischievous face and above all Mama's laughter after we told her a joke or her annoyed face when she caught us doing sneaky things. But this didn't mean that I loved my dad or brother any less than I loved Mama, it was just that from the beginning Mum had always been good at hiding her feelings and that was the first time I had ever seen my own mother cry in front of me. It was the moment in my life when I realised that she is also a human; not a super mum or anything like that. Somewhere along the line I had started to picture her as a very strong woman who'd never crumble under pressure.

On the day that I left East Timor, the air felt clammy and carried along the smell of burning houses. I saw the smoke rising up to the sky and drops of rain fell now and then – I had the silly idea then that the angels in heaven were shedding their tears. Some people on the street looked at us with a vacant expression on their faces, indicating that they had witnessed too much. As I looked around and saw houses burnt beyond recognition, I couldn't fathom why – why anyone would do such a horrible thing.

The following days my brother and I spent time in a 'safe place' in Indonesia, but we were in misery since we had no way to communicate with my parents and brother. I felt lost in a way, because I had absolutely no idea whether or not they managed to survive. The thoughts were too horrible; I couldn't bear thinking about things for more than three seconds and then when I tried to clear my head, I couldn't get the sometimes gruesome image, conjured at the moment of chaos, out of my mind. We kept praying, hoping that God had guided them out of Timor before it had been too late.

On the last day of the second week, we got a call from my dad informing us that they had escaped and were safe and living in Surabaya, Indonesia. They had gotten away about a week and a half after we left. I couldn't put into words how I felt when I heard that they were okay and were waiting for us. The feeling was so intense that I almost felt as though I was going to burst. After all the anxiety and trepidation that I had experienced, this piece of news was the best I had heard in months. The next day, my brother and I left Bali to be reunited with our family. Our family was separated for two weeks, yet it felt like months. I guess I never really did appreciate before the fact that they were always there.

At long last, our family was brought back together in Indonesia. I noticed Mum had lost some weight and her pallid face didn't look at all comforting, Dad had more wrinkles on his face than the last time I saw him and my brother was less of a rascal – although not for long. Eventually it dawned on me – the war had changed us. We were lucky enough not to be caught in the middle of the crossfire – but I had no idea what my parents and brother might have seen on their way out of the country. We tried to steer away from that subject but there was no doubt in my mind that the memory would stay.

Nearing December, we heard that other refugees were returning to Dili and within days, our flight was booked. After the flight, we were dropped off in a deserted place full of unfriendly-looking military men carrying guns – you can imagine what thoughts were running through all of our minds. We spent the next few hours waiting and waiting for our fate to be decided as to whether we would be allowed to go back home. We were hungry and thirsty and worn out after the flight – not a good combination. A few hours later, we were told that we would have to spend a night in a monastery to wait for a bus that would be dropping us off near the border. After that drop off, we would have to arrange our own ride back to our home. It was a terrible day and I remember thinking to myself, *Was this the right decision? What if we don't even make it back to our home?*

In hindsight, what a surprise I would have had if I had actually known that there was no home to return to. When I finally had the chance to visit what used to be our home, I was shocked to see only the walls standing with the rest of the things I recognised peeking out under some rubble and covered in ashes. A sadness overwhelmed me when I saw the music box that my dad gave to me for my tenth birthday, ruined with the half-melted ballerina still inside. I also saw some of my collection of books, beads, comic books and dolls lying around, either scorched by the fire or missing parts and I thought to myself, *I would give anything just to live on like before without this happening at all.* That kind of life was just a couple of months ago, yet it felt like millennia away.

I spent the next few days praying to God that by some miracle our home would be there again. But in the end I realised that a miracle had already happened – we survived. When I thought about some people who had lost their loved ones, I felt ashamed that all I wanted was a house.

Our family spent the next couple of weeks living with a relative all the while planning to rebuild everything. Luckily it didn't take too long for us to build a house with a roof on top of our heads and get the business up and running again. Even when I say that my parents went through a lot, I still consider that an understatement. If I had been the one faced with the challenge of starting my life again from scraps, I'm not even sure that I could ever face up to it. But my parents did it and I couldn't be more proud of them.

Even after all this time I can still remember the faces I saw, the cries I heard, and worst of all the stories told by the people who survived this devastation. I have friends who weren't as lucky to escape unscathed. They had to watch their families, friends and neighbours be killed. They would often describe to me what they saw so vividly that I almost felt as though I had been one of the many who stood and watched the corpses being burned. The '99 massacre was probably the worse incident in the history of East Timor. The people, survivors, are the living testimony to the pain and suffering that we humans are capable of inflicting upon each other. Hundreds died during this massacre – amongst them students, journalists, nuns and many more innocent people.

Lest We Forget: Kutcha's Story

by Kiah McIntyre-Cooper, aged 13

On 26th May 2004 I went to the Sorry Day March in Melbourne. One of my uncles, Mick Edwards, spoke at the march along with a lot of other members of the stolen generation. I really felt sorry for all the people who were taken away from their families just because they were Aboriginal and the government policy of removing Aboriginal children. Although I have known about the stolen generation all my life because of my brother Josh being part of it, I didn't really notice how much it hurt and affected me until I went to this march. Everyone's emotions on that day were so strong. I think almost everyone was hurting, I know I was. The speeches almost broke my heart.

I have to say this is not over and just saying sorry is not enough.

Josh is one of my half brothers. I have never met him. He would be in his mid-thirties now. My dad was only fifteen when Josh was born and his partner at the time was only fourteen. The person I chose to interview for this essay is a man named Kutcha who was one of the many Aboriginal people that were taken away because of his colour and is one of the stolen generation. He is my uncle and here is his story . . .

On one very horrible day at Moulamein, which is about eighty kilometres north east of Swan Hill, a young boy named Kutcha was taken away from his mother and father. He was only eighteen months old and was taken along with five of his brothers and sisters. Six of his other brothers and sisters including Arthur, who is the oldest of the family, weren't taken away. The government took the children to Orana except for Kutcha who was too young for Orana. Orana was in Melbourne, but they took Kutcha to an infant's home across the road from Orana, called Allambie. Kutcha didn't know what he was doing there. He was surrounded by white people. He thought he must be lost or something, so he played up so much that they had to take him across to Orana so he could be with his brothers and sisters.

Some children who were part of the stolen generation had to go through shocking beatings and other abuses. For others there wasn't that much physical beating but more emotional hurting by not being with your mother or father and your uncle and your aunty – 'that's not the way black fellas live, they're meant to be with everyone.'

The very first day Kutcha and his brothers and sisters saw their mother he was six years old. He was sitting in class and over the PA system there was an announcement saying, 'You kids have a visitor at Orana.' But that day no one came to pick them up, so they had to run home and at Orana there was their mother and Kutcha's brother David. Kutcha had never met David before and he didn't know who his mum was. Everyone else was hugging and getting all excited. He said he felt like 'a rabbit in the headlights.' It ended up being a great day, but three or four hours later a caseworker walks up and says, 'Time's up, you have to go.' Kutcha and his family didn't see their mum for another year.

Kutcha told me that at Orana your day was regimented. You get up at the same time every day, have your breakfast, go to school, have your dinner and go to bed, a bit like working, where you clock on and off. People had to learn to build their own little wall around themselves. But everyone knew they weren't meant to be there at Orana. They knew they were meant to be with their families.

About eleven years later, Kutcha was let go from Orana. He came back to Melbourne in 1984. He was about nineteen years old when he did a course called 'Koori Kollij' with a man named Bruce McGuinnis. Gary Foley and his brother Mick were also working there at the time. He didn't really want to do this course but he stayed. There was a little workshop to learn how to be a nurse. They were asking who you were and what you did. It came around to Kutcha and he said, 'My name is Kutcha and I am an unemployed footballer.' It took a very long time to get around the room because there were about sixty people there from all over Australia. Kutcha kept going back every day. They did the course so wherever they came from they could make their own health service because ours, in Victoria, was the very first one. A health service is a medical clinic for Aboriginals which has doctors, dentists and other health professionals. Everyone was being trained to be a nurse. Kutcha learnt about the stolen generation and how he was a part of it. At this time there was a policy called the White Australia policy. This policy occurred because the government wanted there to be no Asians or no dark-skinned people. These laws were passed in the 1920s. There was another policy called assimilation where everyone was to be fair skinned and blue eyed and if you weren't that you were taught to act that way and hopefully one day marry someone of that complexion. Kutcha illustrated this by saying, 'What happens to cordial when you put too much water in it, it turns too weak not just in colour but in flavour, that's what they were trying to do.' They thought that if a black fella married a non-Indigenous girl the colour would be halved but they didn't realise – it doesn't matter about what colour your skin is, it's who you think you are as a person.

Many Australians have learned about the stolen generation through the film *Rabbit Proof Fence*. Kutcha found it very hard to compare the real life experiences of the two aunties to the actors who were in this film. He was concerned that it could be seen to trivialise their experiences. He said when he was watching the film some things were very alike to what he experienced. He couldn't remember all that well about what happened to him because he was only a little boy.

He still hears stories about what happened and he sometimes gets flashbacks of what his father looked like. Sometimes he dreams of his grandparents and he didn't even really get to know them very well at all. He was taken before he could keep a solid image of them in his head. Just like if you see someone and you will not remember if you see them again, but if you see that person over and over you will remember them.

Kutcha often goes out and does talks at primary schools. He is trying his best to inform others about information on the stolen generation. Kutcha is an Aboriginal musician who communicates through his songs. He says it still hurts when he has to go to a funeral and a cousin comes up to him and says, 'Hey coz, what you doin',' and they straight away know who he is but he has no idea who they are. 'And that hurts,' he says.

I chose to call my essay 'Lest We Forget' because I just can't get over the fact that people were taken away from their families. Could you imagine if you were taken away from your family and people were saying, just forget about them, they're old news. I learnt a lot more after doing this essay; I hope you have learnt a bit as well as this is a serious matter that is still hurting a lot of people who never knew their families. My brother and my uncle Kutcha are two of these people.

Eyes Closed: Gashka's Story

by Amelia Easton, aged 15

Many believe that a person's eyes can tell you anything their mouths will not. Gashka, however, also knows how true it is that to hide the past one can simply close one's eyes.

At first, when Gashka came to Australia, she felt lost but excited. She opened her eyes wide in amazement but then shut them tight with fear. She didn't want anyone to know of her past, and was afraid what people would think of her. So, to be able to stay in Australia, to be able to see a life of freedom, she believed she had to keep her eyes firmly closed; that way, the past was closed.

It took six months to process Gashka's claim for asylum; six months of anxious, painstaking waiting, trying to stay out of trouble in Italy and desperately keeping the secret of her relocation to Australia. She dreaded to think what would happen if her 'boss' found out.

Gashka was a happy baby and a happy toddler, and loved to play with her older sister, Ali. Ali always looked after her and protected her. Ali was Gashka's favourite person in the world. Their life, although not always easy, was a happy one, until Gashka was five. Then her mother died giving birth. Her father, who was in the armed forces, was not informed until it was too late.

'I remember my fifth birthday,' Gashka smiles. 'My father was there, wearing one of those funny pointed hats worn at parties. He had a big grin on his face.' Her father left for Bosnia the next day. That was the last time she ever saw him.

After Gashka's mother died, Gashka was placed in an orphanage in Tirane, the capital of Albania, where she stayed until she was fourteen. Ali was taken away too, but Gashka does not know where she went. She speculates that Ali was placed in a different orphanage but does not know for sure. Ali was seven the last time they saw each other.

'I hated those walls, the big, white walls that were now black with filth and red with blood. The roof was inches from our head. We lived almost in closets . . . Nobody there but the matrons, who beat us. Locked away until the day we were sold or just died. There was no escape.'

Though in 1993, when Gashka was fourteen, she found one.

'I ran, ran so fast . . . I didn't stop. When I got to the refugee camp I collapsed. Even this place, so foreign, was more home to me.'

Gashka's collapse was partly due to relief but also exhaustion. When examined by the camp doctor, however, it was revealed that Gashka was in bad shape. The doctors thought it amazing that she had managed to run so far with pneumonia. Her fever was now so high after the ordeal that she was delirious. It took three weeks to recover from the illness, but the doctor was there by her side every day.

The camp, on the outskirts of Tirane, had been set up for those affected by the Yugoslavian and Bosnian conflicts. Bosnia was where her father was serving. Thousands of people were crammed into camps just like the one in Tirane, with no possessions and many missing family.

'Those camps, they were like little villages, all the houses made of tents,' Gashka recalls. 'So little space, but we got to know each other. For once, I had people I trusted. It was so cold without Ali, but I met someone who helped me through it.'

One of these people was the doctor, with whom Gashka had formed a bond since falling ill. He had looked after her well, and she had come to look up to him like a father. One day, he had a proposition for Gashka.

'He sat me down, and he told me: "Gashka, you pretty babik girl ('babik' is Ukrainian for 'baby'), look at you. You are like my daughter. I will take you to Italy, and look after you!" And he did take me to Italy.'

For about a month, Gashka was fed and clothed well. 'He treated me like a princess,' she says. He took her to Rome, Pisa and Venice, and showered her with gifts. She felt loved for the first time in years. They then journeyed to his home in Florence.

One day, it all changed, at a meeting with one of the doctor's business associates.

'He said, "There's somebody . . . You meet them. You will like him." I met him. I didn't like him . . . I didn't know him. But I was told, "Just get to know him, my babik girl. Everything will be all right."'

Gashka remembers the next evening having dinner at this new man's house. She never found out his name.

'The doctor, he spoke to the stranger in Italian, and I did not understand. The stranger handed over some money, lots of money. They both smiled and left me in the room. I never saw the doctor, my friend, again.'

It didn't take long before everything became clear. Gashka had been sold into a prostitution ring. There she stayed, in a Florence alleyway, seen by only 'the filthiest of men,' in 'nothing but my underwear.' There were other girls, a few from the Balkans region, others mostly from Russia or Africa, but no one Gashka could turn to. So there, in the backstreets of Florence, she stayed for three cold years, ashamed at herself but forced to keep going.

'The man, we were never allowed to look up at him. We must keep our eyes low. We were "dirt" he says. He watches us every day, our every move, taking all our money. We work hard, ashamed, but having no choice, and in the end we have nothing. We have less than what we start with, because now we have no dignity, now we are worthless.'

In 1996, when Gashka was seventeen, the Italian Government was informed of this particular prostitution ring. Nine girls, including Gashka, were taken and put into care. The oldest of the girls was eighteen, the youngest eleven.

In February that year, Gashka filed a claim for asylum in Australia. For six months the Australian Government, together with the Italian Embassy, helped provide her with the necessities she needed. She worked as a washerwoman, doing laundry in one of her rooms for other people. There was not much pay, but she was eager to please the Embassy by showing she would work hard if given the opportunity in Australia. After six months, that opportunity came.

In August, she received the good news.

'The worker at the Embassy, I remember Helen was her name, she read the letter to me. I have learnt Italian now, and I was so proud to understand those words. I felt strong. I was so happy, and I cried.'

Within a week of asylum being granted, Gashka arrived in Perth, and after another two weeks, she came to Adelaide.

'At first, I was so scared. I didn't want to talk or to tell. I closed my eyes a lot so people wouldn't know. I felt different and ashamed of my past. But people here, they may not know what it's like, but they understand.'

Gashka prefers only to talk to a few people about her ordeal but also wants her story to be heard.

'No one deserves it. I want people to be aware. I hate to remember, but I don't want to forget. Because if I do, I forget my strength and my courage. I want to tell others that they have courage too. I know now that it wasn't my fault, so I no longer have to keep it a secret.

'I no longer walk around with my eyes closed.'

Honey: The Story of an Asylum Seeker's Cat

by Luke D Ryan, aged 11

I come from Manus Island. There was a man on this island. He fled his country and tried to get to Australia but didn't quite get there. So he came to this island and some people detained him. He had to wait there until they let him into Australia.

This man began to look lonelier with every passing day. So I sneaked into the detention camp, as the humans called it. I walked straight up to him; he looked at me, then picked me up. I could not speak his language so I just looked at him, a simple way of saying, 'Do you want to be friends?'

He said, 'My name is Aladdin Sisalem, but just call me Aladdin. I'm going to call you Honey.' I very much liked the name he gave me. Over the next couple of hours Aladdin told me all about himself and also said how nice it was to talk to somebody.

We really had to depend on each other, Aladdin and I. There was nobody else in the detention centre. Yet we kept ourselves occupied. We played all types of games. My favourite one was when Aladdin rolled up some newspaper and we kicked it around and I'm really good at it now. He was also a good story-teller (well, at least I think so – humans might like different things in stories from cats). At night, and other times too, we would roll up together and he would tell me a story.

This detention centre would have been terribly depressing if we had not had each other. We just became best mates. We

135

could understand each other without needing to even talk (or, in my case, meow). By this time I could dribble the rolled up newspaper the length of the room and Aladdin said, 'Wow.'

About ten months after we first met, Aladdin got a visa. The people who ran the detention centre wouldn't let him bring me. How pathetic – what's so bad about a cat? So Aladdin went off to Australia. As he was about to leave, I waved a paw and then burst into tears. Yet I thought I would see him again one day. Cats just know these things.

Some interested people listened to Aladdin about us and agreed we should be together. They raised money so we could be reunited. All this for me! They wanted ME to come to Australia! Meow! Meow!

As I write this, I am in a place called Papua New Guinea. I will then travel to Australia.

~

The day has come!

I travelled on a big machine called an aeroplane. The two scariest parts of the journey were when the plane went up into the sky and when it came back down. Imagine a flying cat!

I'm so excited. They told me after three months I'll get to see and play with Aladdin in Australia! 'Meow, Meow!' I exclaimed.

I really believe, to use a human expression, that Aladdin and I are going to live happily ever after.

My Own Journey: Understanding Multiculturalism

by Edith Tom, aged 14

She stands at one side of the crowded platform, next to the bag of her daughter's luggage. It has fallen open, strewing its contents across the concrete. The daughter stands a few steps away, embarrassed and impatient, pretending to examine the train timetables pinned up on the wall. 'Mum!' the girl hisses, glancing around the platform to see if anyone has noticed the spilt luggage. Her mother sighs and wishes that her daughter would someday understand. A family walks past, stepping onto a woollen jacket that had been washed the day before so that a daughter would not be cold on her school camp. She hears them whisper in the foreign language and blushes when she comprehends their meaning – 'Bloody Chinese.'

I am a fourteen-year-old Australian-born Chinese-Timorese girl, and I'm fortunate enough to live in a country where people don't have to worry about strangers invading their homes in the middle of the night or bombs falling from the sky. We live in a blessed country filled with opportunities and with a diverse range of cultures. Up until two years ago, I had no idea about the importance of this. It wasn't until I had to write a speech about the topic of multiculturalism that I began to realise what the word 'culture' really means.

My speech read: 'Good morning, ladies and gentlemen. Multiculturalism is the integration of several different cultures into one society.' But is it really? To me, multiculturalism was simply a term that could be used when describing certain societies, nothing more. To tell you the truth, I had never really been interested in my own culture let alone the cultures of others. Attending my Chinese language classes once a week was a tedious ritual that I was always complaining about, and I never really had the time nor patience to listen to my parents' stories about their homeland.

However, it was finally time for me to learn more about different cultures if I was to finish my speech, and so I set out on my own journey – to learn about the journeys of others.

There has always been something about the ability of a novel to create a believable world that captivates me and fills me with awe. For me, there is no greater ecstasy than living a story that has leaped out from its pages, enchanting its reader and forever embedding itself in a memory. But for all the books I have read, there have only been the rare few that even come close to creating this ecstasy.

And so, as I began my search for the stories of others, I never expected to be affected as strongly as I was. I was more deeply moved by a few lines of imperfect English than I could ever be from reading a lifetime's worth of books. I had finally discovered the words that could stir my innermost emotions. Perhaps it was because these stories inspired me, or maybe it was just because I felt such a connection in that these were real accounts of real people. All around me, I found amazing stories of courage, danger, heartache and hope – even when it seemed that hope was impossible. Even in my small group of closest friends, there were people who had fled their countries because there was no longer a safe place to hide; people who had their friends and relatives taken away for no real reason; and people who had had their father held at gunpoint.

In the midst of all the stories of struggle, escaping and over-coming hardships to rebuild a life, I finally found the story that would complete the last chapter of my journey's chronicles. Although this isn't a story of oppression, despair or violence, it is a story that conveys the indescribable pain of losing something that can never be replaced, and the emotional suffering that teaches us to be stronger. You may ask how I was able to come across such a story. My answer will not be, 'after years of interviewing people and attending forums.' I found this story as soon as I took the time to listen.

My mother left East Timor to migrate with an older sister to Taiwan so that she could complete her education. It's scary to think that when they left their family behind, my mother and aunt weren't any older than I am now, yet I can't comprehend what it must have been like and how they coped. My mother told me that the schools in East Timor didn't have enough teachers to provide any education beyond the primary years. It was a year after my mother had graduated from her university and had started teaching in Taipei that the conflict in East Timor meant that her family could no longer stay there. Her father, my grandfather, arranged for the entire family to migrate to Australia to join two of my uncles, so that the family could finally be reunited again. Sadly, my grandfather died of liver cancer before his wish could be fulfilled. Although my mother was happy in Taiwan with a well-paid job and stable lifestyle, she gave up her own opportunities to migrate to Australia under her father's wishes, and so that the future generation would have an easier way of life. She arrived in Darwin in 1981, leaving behind friends, her students, boxes of books and other treasured items that are now lost, and happy memories. Soon after arriving in Darwin, my mother moved to Sydney and began working as a sewing machinist. What moves me most about my mother's story is that she tells it without a single complaint or without a hint of the pain that she must feel. But every time her eyes glaze over as she tells me about the past, I feel the pain that she must have felt when giving up everything that was important to her, just so that we could grow up in a safe and stable country where learning can be fun and life is filled with opportunities. I think about the contrast between the life she could have had in Taiwan and the difficulty of starting over in a new country, with a new language to learn and among strangers. And I can't possibly imagine the fear that my mother, and so many others like her, would have felt. I don't think I will ever truly understand what my mother feels. But I have finally learnt to embrace my culture. Suddenly, I find myself looking forward to every Saturday morning that I can spend learning about my background.

Most importantly, I have uncovered the true meaning of emotional strength. To be emotionally strong doesn't mean staying tearless after getting dumped by your boyfriend. It means still having the strength to cry when everyone around you can't cry anymore because all you face is numbness, desperation and despair. I guess that's why it makes me so angry when people make a racist remark without realising how much migrants or refugees have had to go through. It angers me that people are judged by where they come from and the way they look, rather than the person that they are.

That's why we need to work together to eradicate racism and to establish a world that embraces multiculturalism. And the meaning of multiculturalism? I did finish my speech, and I decided that multiculturalism is a lot more than a whole heap of different cultures. It's about equality, peace, tolerance and strength – as one. If we could create a multicultural society built upon tolerance and giving, we would live in a perfect world. I remember that the first thing I was taught was to share. If we were to do just that, the poverty in our world would be eradicated, eliminating the need for crime. With tolerance, there would no longer be hatred. Without hatred, how can there possibly be war? Multiculturalism can be a powerful tool that brings all the different people of the world together, breaking down barriers and uniting us all. United, we could achieve so much more.

Creating a multicultural world in itself would be the greatest achievement in our history. And yet, as daunting a task as it may seem, all it takes is something as simple as a smile. Each and every one of us has the power to bring Australia and the world that much closer to making the dream of multiculturalism – a dream of equality, peace, tolerance and strength – a reality.

Finding Home:
Allan Tan's Story

by Jay Higson-Coleing, aged 11

I was wandering through the crowd at the Mindil Beach markets; I had only been in Darwin a few months, so why did it feel so familiar? Was it the smells from the Asian food stalls, was it the crowds or noise, or was it the hot, steamy air? I stopped and thought: all of this is like my old home in Cambodia. My mind shot back to a time I had tried to forget.

I was four years old when my parents were murdered by the Khmer Rouge during the civil war. Over the next few years I remember that my brothers and sisters were forced to work seven days a week. Life was very hard then but we survived.

It was during the Vietnamese occupation of Cambodia. I was about nine years old when my eldest brother, Huy, made the decision to leave. After years of suffering under the Khmer Rouge, many could not face the uncertainty and were afraid of what lay ahead. My two brothers and two sisters and I left with only the clothes we were wearing and I remember being barefoot. We were not the only ones. I remember lots of people running, trying to escape what was happening in Cambodia by crossing the border into Thailand. It was a dangerous journey, we could only travel at night and we had to sleep on the side of the road. I remember hiding and always having to be quiet. One time I coughed and my brother put his hand over my mouth because

I was being too noisy. Even crying babies had to be kept quiet. We had to beg for food and I was always hungry and thirsty. I was very scared and confused so I just followed and did what my brothers and sisters told me to. The area near the border was full of landmines and many people were killed. I will never forget the smell of the swollen bodies. It was the worst time of my life.

When we eventually made it to Thailand we were put in a refugee camp. At last we felt safe. There were fences around the camp and we weren't allowed to leave but we had food to eat and shelter, so I was happier. I don't know exactly how many people were in the camp but it was like a little bamboo city. Life in the camp wasn't that bad. In the morning I went to school and in the afternoon I could play with other kids but still this wasn't a home. Everyone in the camp was waiting to go to other countries like France, America or Australia. Once a week we would check the noticeboard to see if our names were on the list. We were there for four long years. At last in 1983 we were able to come to Australia under the Unaccompanied Minors Program.

It was a real shock being in a new country with different people and a different language. It was hard learning about everything all over again. Everything was so new: the culture, the food, the people, everything. I lived with my brothers, Huy and Sean, and my sisters, Anita and Amanda, in a one-bedroom flat in Adelaide. We had to sleep practically on top of each other but I didn't mind because I didn't know any different. When you are young you just learn to accept things. At first I went to a special language school where I met other children from Cambodia as well as others who couldn't speak English. The Indochinese Refugee Association sent a social worker once a week to check on us to see how we were getting on.

After about a year of going to the special language school I was allowed to go to a proper high school and start Year Seven. I was thirteen years old at the time but things weren't like I imagined. Everyday I got bullied and teased. I remember every day I used to cry and cry. People made me feel so bad about myself. By Year Nine my English was much better so I was starting to learn how to cope with the bullying and how to talk back.

I've been in Australia for twenty years now. I've achieved a lot. I have a career, a home but most of all a place where I feel safe. Australia really is a lucky country.

As I sat on the beach watching the sunset I realised that this was the closest I'd ever been to my old home but, although Cambodia will always be a part of me, Australia is my home.

My Experience as a Refugee

by Lual Makuei Deng, aged 21

But what exactly is a refugee? For the sake of those people who don't know, a refugee is a person who has been forced to leave his or her homeland in order to escape persecution, war or a natural disaster. But to me this is only a small portion of the definition.

Somewhere in the land known to the world as Sudan is my home. I fled the country on my own, not knowing where I was going but fleeing as far I could from the big booms of the weapons I heard. I had two siblings who were older than me. Six was my age, but I was strong enough to stand my ground and defend myself from the opportunists who wanted to snatch all the food that I had. We were given a cup of maize to last us for three days by the rebel government who claimed to be responsible for us. My mother and father disappeared from me and this hurts until this day, though we were reunited years later. Did they do it on purpose or were they just escaping for their lives? Should they have died for my sake or not? Questions are still unanswered for me.

As far as I'm concerned, living as a refugee is the last thing I would like my family, relatives or friends to experience. First I could not find my parents, siblings and relatives. I was alone with thousands of other confused children. We had to walk from Sudan to Ethiopia on foot; hunger was unbearable, no drops of water to drink let alone for hygiene; the long walk of twenty hours a day was torturing. I ran out of breath, strength and so decided to rest for a little while under the shade of a tree. Then all of a sudden a soldier who was roaming on his own saw me and asked me, 'What's the matter son?' He wasn't convincing and I did not trust him, so I said nothing at all. He was not happy with my reaction and he didn't look in good shape either. But he saved me from that moment when he told me that he knew my parents and knew that they were waiting for me at the end of the journey. I gulped in the air and life began in me once again. After about seven days of walking there was no sign of ending to the journey and I did things that I will never forget in my lifetime. When I was ready to urinate I had to store the drops of my urine and retain them hopefully for the next moment when I needed water to walk. All of the children were forced to do this in order to survive. Yes, I did drink my own urine to save the life that I regret living.

We had to face many challenges and one of the most dangerous was crossing a river that was flowing fast and with wild crocodiles in it. Lucky for me my brother gave me swimming lessons that seemed to be a lot of fun at the time but saved me that day. We finally arrived at a placed called Pinydud. The natives were not friendly but we didn't mind because some of the older people went out to hunt and they shared their food with us. Although we had some food it was not enough to survive and we also had to fight off the natives who wanted to steal what little we had. I was lucky that I had an older brother there who protected me and made sure I got a little food. Many other children were not as lucky and they were killed, as they did not have the strength to fight.

Some of the other children also died because of the disease that rose when we were in the town. A few days later, an organisation known as the United Nations came to rescue us from the pain, suffering and hunger that we were undergoing. They gave us food, clothing, blankets and sleeping tents to protect us from the sun, rain and wind. These were the only people so far we had known to care for us.

In Ethiopia we had the first taste of discrimination in our entire lives. They called us 'Lama' which meant blacks. This felt like a needle in my heart. And just when I thought my nightmares were over, we had to flee again to Kenya because the country that we were in was involved in a civil war. Although we shared the same border and they knew about what happened in Sudan, they did not take any notice or try to learn from our experiences. I didn't want this to happen to them because they would face the hardship that we experienced.

Staying in Kenya was hard as well, because we had to face high temperatures of forty-five degrees during the day and thirty in the night. When we tried to flee from the desert region, we were harassed by the local police. They told us to pay them some amount of money otherwise they would lock us in the prison, even though we had all the required documents to be in the country. Sometimes they even told me that it was God that was punishing us as was foretold in the Holy Scripture. This altered my view of religion to a negative perspective.

When I was reunited with my family members, I didn't want to see them or talk to them because they had left me in the wilderness alone. That was the mentality of a seven-year-old boy. On the other hand, I was glad to see them alive since some of the kids who were with me lost their parents in the war and needed someone to take care of them. This made me change my mind and to accept their presence since it wasn't all my free will but by Almighty will.

As we stayed in the refugee camp known as Kakuma we managed to apply for resettlement in Australia and, thank God, we were accepted. When we came to Australia, I thought all was good but to my surprise I received discrimination in various levels. It looks like all my life has been nothing but bad and I don't know what is good for me. Maybe my homeland that I was born in, but then why did I have to leave it? Maybe I should have died like my other relatives in the proper land? Or wait for death when I couldn't walk anymore. Being a refugee is never a good thing, it will guarantee you racism no matter what race you come from and it will deprive you of humanity. When you see a refugee have heart, for what they have experienced is of the lowest pits of humanity.

My Country is Afghanistan ...

by Fabienne Trevere, aged 14

This story is about Nahid, an Afghan girl living in Australia. Nahid came here by boat, so I suppose, technically, that makes her an 'unauthorised arrival.' Some people would even go so far as to call her a 'queue jumper' or 'illegal immigrant.' To me, she is simply a refugee, a person who came to this country to seek protection from the Taliban, a group of brutal extremists who ruled her country until just a few years ago.

Many people, in fact almost everyone I know, would consider Nahid's life in recent years to have been unbelievably difficult: a year spent virtually imprisoned in the house of a Pakistani smuggler, before travelling in a boat that was barely seaworthy from Indonesia to Australia, where she spent another nine months in the Port Hedland detention centre – her story, inevitably, is bound up with the issue of mandatory detention of asylum seekers.

But let me be clear, I have not written this story to make any sort of point. I have written it only to give an account of one of the most courageous, passionate and inspiring girls I have ever been fortunate enough to meet.

'My country is Afghanistan,' she tells me. Afghanistan: that land-locked country of rugged mountains and plains, situated in the heart of Central Asia. Such a romantic description, however, obscures the fact that Afghanistan's strategic location has long been as much a curse as a blessing. For centuries, the country has been a target of foreign powers, and its recent history has continued to be characterised by war and civil unrest.

Not that Nahid loves her country any less because of this. On the contrary, she continually talks about just how wonderful Afghanistan is and what a beautiful city Herat is, or was. Herat, Afghanistan's second largest city, is where Nahid grew up. It has a history extending back over 2500 years, and it *had* a reputation as a centre of art, learning and trade. Successive warlords have attempted to put an end to that way of life – and the Taliban were neither the first nor the last of these rulers.

Nahid tells me that Herat for her was a peaceful city until the Taliban took over. After that, she says, life became impossible for everyone. It is difficult to imagine that life could change so suddenly. But that was the reality for most people in Afghanistan, and especially for women. In just a few days, all of the freedom they had progressively gained over the past few decades was lost.

Formed by religious students who had fled Afghanistan during the Soviet invasion, the Taliban introduced repressive policies against all sectors of society. They banned everything they considered to be frivolous or not in accordance with their own narrow interpretation of the Islamic religion – such as wedding parties, picnics, toys, photographs, laughing in public, applause, make-up – and they brutally enforced these decrees. Particularly harsh were their edicts concerning women. The Taliban prohibited education for girls and forced women to quit their jobs. They denied women access to medical care, imposed a restrictive dress code and basically condemned women to a form of house arrest.

A woman walking with her children was whipped by Taliban guards with a car aerial because she had let her veil slip . . . a woman was stoned to death after being found guilty of adultery . . . the end of a

*woman's thumb was cut off by the Taliban because she was caught
wearing nail varnish . . . a woman was shot as she stepped outside
her house to seek medical care for her child . . .*

Nahid never went to school in Afghanistan. Just at the time she
was about to begin, the Taliban took over. So her father arranged
for the local teacher to hold private study sessions in their home.
'I didn't learn as much as I would have in school, but it was better
than doing nothing,' she says. 'Of course, it was very dangerous
for the teacher. If the Taliban had found out, she would have
been killed.'

The family decided to leave Afghanistan. There were many
reasons for doing so. Nahid's parents were worried about her two
brothers, both of them almost thirteen. As soon as boys turned
thirteen in Afghanistan, the Taliban would force them into the
army. Nahid herself was also in danger. As soon as girls in
Afghanistan began to mature, they would be hassled by the
Taliban and by men who wanted to marry them. Many young
girls were stolen off the street and coerced into marriage.

Despite the life she was forced to live in Afghanistan, Nahid
was sad to have to leave the country of her birth. After all, it was
the place where she had grown up, and everyone she knew and
loved lived there. But Nahid had many dreams, none of which
could come true for her in Afghanistan. Over there she was
too busy just trying to survive and had no time to think of her
future. 'Every day,' she told me, 'I would wake up and wonder,
"Am I going to lose my parents? Am I going to lose someone I
love?" And I did. A lot of people I loved were killed over there.
That's what it was like.'

After making the decision to leave Afghanistan, the family went
first to Pakistan. Nahid's father wanted to go to Australia, where
he would be able to receive protection as a refugee. He believed
that once his case for asylum was accepted, his wife and children

would be allowed to join him. And so, like many other hopeful asylum seekers, he entrusted his life to a smuggler who had promised him a new life in Australia.

Nahid, along with her mother and her brothers, had to wait for almost a year in Pakistan in the care of another smuggler, while her father's case for asylum was processed. For most of the time, they were confined to a single room of the smuggler's house. The door of this room was kept locked.

Upon arrival in Australian territory Nahid's father had been put in detention, where he stayed until he was given a visa – a Temporary Protection Visa. Recipients of these visas cannot bring any family to join them in Australia and lose their visa if they travel outside the country.

As he was unable to sponsor them to join him, her father suggested the rest of the family come to Australia in the same way he had – by boat. They did, and were immediately put in detention, in Port Hedland.

Throughout that long journey across the sea, Nahid says it was the thought of Australia that gave her strength. To her, Australia represented safety and security, things she had lived without for most of her life. Coming to Australia, she believed, would free her from all the hardships and suffering she had faced so far.

The detention centre in Port Hedland was established in 1991, following an influx of asylum seekers. In recent years it has been the site of many violent riots and there have been numerous claims from human rights groups of physical abuse against detainees. Nahid remembers the terrifying fires and witnessing two men attempt suicide. Her younger brother watched a man pour hot water over himself.

She also remembers the toothache that started bothering her soon after her arrival. 'The pain gradually became worse,' she says, 'until I couldn't sleep at night. It felt like my whole head was splitting.' Everyday she would ask the medical staff at the detention centre for help, but all they could do was give her a Panadol and tell her to wait for the dentist's visit.

> *All centres reported managing demand for dental services as a major problem. Because of advanced dental problems in the detainee community, most visiting dentists spent all their time on pain relief and extractions, with no time left over to provide children with the preventative dental care they needed.*
>
> From A Last Resort? The National Inquiry into
> Children in Immigration Detention

Nahid found it difficult to cope in detention. She felt that all those things that had given her hope during the boat trip from Indonesia had suddenly been taken away from her, leaving her with nothing but questions. Why were she and her family being detained? And why couldn't she see her father? She didn't feel safe in detention; she certainly didn't feel free. But not knowing when it would all end, not having that sense of security she had longed for: that, she says, was the worst of it.

'When I was given my visa I was so happy! You, or anyone else, cannot imagine how happy I was at that moment! I felt like a bird, a free bird who is able to fly high, high and higher!'

Although Nahid is right when she says no one else could possibly understand her feelings of happiness when she was formally recognised as a refugee, her words give a general idea. Hearing those words almost causes me to forget everything she has told me previously about the lower points of her life. Her feeling of joy is infectious, and I can't help but be impressed by her positive attitude towards life. Nahid comes across as a soft-spoken girl, however I don't doubt for a moment the tremendous inner strength she must have relied upon to come as far as she has.

After being released from detention, Nahid was able to reunite with her father. Happily, the separation of almost two years caused no damage to their relationship, and they are now once again very close. Her family moved to Sydney, and, within a week, Nahid's father had enrolled her in school. She is now studying hard, hoping to finish her education and go on to university.

Nahid assures me that one day she would love to go back to Afghanistan, but not any time soon. Not until her country is at peace, and the rights of women, in particular, are more widely respected.

Unfortunately Nahid doesn't have the luxury of choosing when she would like to return. Since her Temporary Protection Visa expired she has lived in constant fear of being sent back to Afghanistan and losing her new friends and loved ones all over again.

I suppose it's not surprising that Nahid's greatest wish at the moment is just to remain living here in Australia with her family. But she is quick to add that she would like to become 'well-known' and that, of course, she would like to work to help people in any way she can.

It's at this time I remember reading that a Taliban official once said, 'We do not need women to work. What positive role can they play in society? What is the impact of their roles? We do not need women. They should stay in their houses.' I disagree, and I know Nahid would as well. As anyone who has met her would tell you, Nahid has *a lot* to contribute to society, now and in the future, both in Afghanistan and in Australia!

Hank's Story

by Carla Johnson, aged 16

It's so clear: I can remember just how it used to be. Just sitting here, on the same log as when I was just a kid. Uncle used to show me how to catch my favourite, the bird. Mum said we want to be here forever and it would stay like that. I liked it when Mum talked like that. Even her grandma's mum lived here.

The ocean in view for as far as you can see. Who would have thought how life could change in an instant? Looking around, I remember so much, where we used to live. Our sheds, I realise now, were simple. But back then it was like a castle to me. Where we used to play, eat, hunt, fish. I loved fishing; we would all go out together. See who could get the biggest one . . . I'd always win. I loved it . . . It's all gone now though.

Never realised how lucky I was, carefree. The world was so small back then. The island was my home, my family, our land. Surrounded by the ocean, happy with life, I knew I belonged, everyone did.

The best bit's the tucker, it's a smorgasbord, more than you'd want.

My favourite's the bird. Put ya' hand down the hole, grab the neck and crack.

They are good . . . Better than KFC crap. But when the hole is cold . . . you gotta . . . get ya hand out . . . real quick . . . You know what lives down them cold holes. They were big ones too . . . long as, and fatter than ya leg. Fish too. Wait for the tide to go out and you'd get 'em in the pools. Just pick 'em up in your hands.

Someone must 'ave thought it was too good here . . . Wanted it for themselves . . . They packed us up and moved us on . . . Herded us to Tassie.

Paddocks, fences, we were trapped like animals. But we see none. Not like home. No sea for the fish. Ohh . . . I can still smell a good bird . . . That long warm hole and crack . . . Whack them on a fire and they are good. I miss that. Luck's all gone.

No birds in Tassie. Canned peas, canned ham, canned corn, sick again.

Mum found it toughest. She was the Rock on the island. She knew it all. Strip a bird in seconds. Saw her catch a brownie with her bare hands. She didn't do much back in Tassie though, the Rock. She got the sickest. Stayed in bed all day sometimes.

The same people that sent us here think we should go to school. That's not the bad part. It's history that sucks. They don't know history like I do.

They told me, 'Truganinni was the last Tasmanian Aboriginal.'

I stood up for my family. I told them. I told them who we are. But they wouldn't listen so I asked, 'Who are them blackfellas in my kitchen?'

They answered with six of the best. I took those six and never went back. But . . . Who are them blackfellas in my kitchen? What does that make me? A shadow.

Nothing seemed right. The Rock . . . she was struggling. The family fell apart. On the island she had a face. That's gone now. Stayed in bed all day heaps.

You know, my brother got sick again too. Real sick. Had to go to Melbourne to get the right stuff. Flew him across the Strait they did. Mum was nervous. She was looking after him. That was all right 'til she got on the plane. Rode her in the back they did. Back there with the wildlife. No seats for the blackfella. She had to stick her head through the door to breathe warm air. She hasn't got a birth certificate 'cause she was born on the island.

But . . . 'Truganinni was the last Tasmanian Aboriginal.'

I got married. Father of one. She's gorgeous and so is the little one, dark like Mum and me. I love her.

Football's good in Tassie. More teams than on the island. We were doing all right. Won more than we lost, too . . . Enraged, I bashed him . . . Who was that bastard to call my wife a 'nigga lover'? The racist prick pressed charges . . . I felt a suspended sentence was worth it.

The Rock didn't think so, things got bad for her. Sick and needy and fed up, she thought that black and white couldn't mix. Took her shadow with her she did.

'Grog don't like blackfellas,' but it had all the answers I needed.

It captured me. I'm no good on the grog and very ugly after ten years of it.

Life crumbled. Family, friends and me. I missed here.

There were two roads to walk down and one road to choose. Should I dissolve my shadow too? No one respected me. We were treated like dogs for being black – Aboriginal.

But . . . 'Trugannini was the last Aboriginal.'

Love struck me again. It was different. It was lifting.

Confident to work and filled with meaning, I needed a house. Somewhere to live. It was a beauty too. Three bedrooms, garage and a magic garden. My wife had it all sorted over the phone. I went in to pick up the keys and they said, 'Sorry, it's been rented,' they said. No keys for a blackfella.

But . . . 'Trugannini was the last Aboriginal.'

I've fixed it all now. I've ditched the grog and learnt to read and write. Thirty-five years old when I went back to school. People want to hear what I say. I tell them all about the way we Aboriginals live. I employ uncles, aunties and brothers and sister. I've found myself, who I used to be. Who I am now. It's bought my family back together. We found culture again. The black, yellow and red flies high at my house. Most people listen but others don't want to hear.

Business is good. A heap of tourists and the art is selling well. But one prick . . . He reckons he could trade me two grand of dope for a painting. Are people stupid? What do they reckon? 'Cause I'm black I smoke dope. I told him where to go. I know he wouldn't offer a white man dope in his shop.

I looked smart, sophisticated, briefcase and everything. Three grand ready to buy my computer. Then in the shop this bitch shrieked, 'Eh you . . . Leave your briefcase at the door.' Her voice would peel your skin. Felt like a brownie on hot coals . . . 'Yes, you with the briefcase, leave it behind the counter.'

I tried to explain. I'd seen kids walking round with school bags on, enough room for a whole CD player in them. Would she listen? I'm black. No, of course not. Never been back to that shop again.

They do it when they don't even realise. You'd think the minister would know. The Minister for Tourism invited me to make a speech. I like doing them. Good for business and for us Aboriginal people. But you'd think he'd know. He introduced me as a 'half Aboriginal' . . . What is a half caste? I stood up on stage . . . side on . . . and said, 'This is my Aboriginal half.' The audience knew what I meant. They laughed. I hope the minister learnt. He'd probably done history. Learnt that Trugannini was the last Tasmanian Aboriginal.

Life is great now, travelling, teaching and still learning. It has its downs, but I have support, great family, great friends and great business. I still think about here though. Will always miss it. I know what life is all about here.

Doing what I do for my people makes me proud. I am noticed. Not just a shadow anymore. I have found my face and I know where it's looking.

The Earth is Here for All of Us: Ahmad's Story

by Nitya Dambiec, aged 17

'These men, they would kill human beings like cows or sheep,' Ahmad tells me. 'After killing them they would be happy, and they would laugh about it.'

He was talking about Saddam's men, who had captured and hung his uncle, and then come for him. Ahmad, who is Kurdish, a persecuted minority in Iraq, was studying car mechanics in Baghdad when he was taken by Saddam's Ba'ath officials to be locked in a room, questioned and beaten.

'They beat me here,' Ahmad shows me, 'and here, and here. They broke these bones, in my ribs, and my head. Then they put acid on me,' and he shows me the scars on the front of his shoulder. Human life to these men held no value; they preached religion as an excuse for inhumanity. They had killed Ahmad's uncle, and, although he had done nothing to threaten Saddam's regime, there was no reason for them not to kill Ahmad as well.

'It was eight in the morning when I was taken to the house,' Ahmad tells me, 'and three the next morning when I escaped.' The older man who was with him told him how to get away. You had to use your arm to break the window and push the glass with your body. As long as you have your legs, then you can run. Your arm is not important.

The glass shattered and Ahmad's body bled, his yellow T-shirt red with blood. Yes, he had his legs, but they weren't about to take him anywhere. The morning was dark and he was alone on the roadside bleeding. Cars drove by. Two, then three. The fourth car stopped to pick him up. 'This was a very good man who picked me up,' Ahmad tells me, 'I will never forget this man.' About the other men, the men who beat him and hung his uncle, I am told: 'I don't want to practise hatred. I don't want to feel hatred inside my heart.'

My mother's hands were shaking as she told me to go

Ahmad arrived at his family home in the early hours of the morning, his body still bleeding from the glass and broken from being beaten. His mother cleaned the blood, and, although he would need operations, he could not go to hospital, because his family's neighbours were members of Saddam's Ba'ath Party, and he would soon be recaptured if he chose to stay. Within half an hour he was gone, and this time his legs had no choice but to carry him; to carry him far, far away from his family, never to see them again.

'My mother's hands were shaking like this,' Ahmad says and shows me. '"You have to go," she said, and I never saw my family again.' There is a pause. 'Sorry,' he says, wanting to tell the story, but stopping to dry the tears of sad and painful memories from his eyes. Ahmad was my age when this happened, and I try to imagine my mother's hands shaking, or my friends' mother's hands, as they say a final farewell to their son or daughter after having cleaned them of blood and not knowing how long they'll survive. I try to imagine that my relatives were hung, my school friends tortured and beaten, even without having political connections, just for being who they were. Imagine having to run with broken bones and nowhere to go, running far, far away . . .

The land of no crying and no laughing

'I had to be strong,' Ahmad tells me as he continues. Running for days, he ate and drank very little until arriving at a forest between

Iraq, Syria and Turkey. He had no food left and lived by fishing. He lived in the forest for many months, totally alone, until he was found by a dog, a German Shepherd, who followed him and became his friend. It was a different sort of living, living like this. There was no crying during this time, Ahmad tells me, and no laughing either. It was living only until the next day, worrying about what would happen tomorrow, or the next hour, worrying about whether there would be soldiers with guns who would beat him and kill him.

Time passed, the sun would rise and set, and each new day would come and go. On one of these days, Ahmad saw some people. First he hid from them, but they had no guns. Then he talked to them, and they came to know one another and lived together for a while. Ahmad managed to make contact with his dad, who sent him different items that he needed – clothes, and two hundred American dollars. It was time to move again, and, with the money he had been given, Ahmad travelled through Syria to Jordon.

You cannot buy a Kurdish passport
On arrival in Jordon, Ahmad's family sent him seven thousand American dollars. This was the last contact he was to have with them. Even a little money could get you a long way, but no amount of money could turn around the trials of Ahmad's life, could bring back his family, give him a home, or change the fact that he was a refugee.

What the money could do was buy him a passport. Fake, yes, but he could not stay in Jordon and there was no other way out. As he explained, you can't apply for a Kurdish passport, because the Kurdish people have no country, and Saddam's government wasn't about to give him anything.

When he handed over his passport at the airport, the Jordanian policeman started to laugh. Did he know that the photo was a fake? But Ahmad couldn't see how, it was so similar to his own face. 'Your face looks like the face of my brother,' the policeman said, and waved him through the checkout.

The boat where you forget yourself, and learn something about love

From Jordan Ahmad flew to Kuala Lumpur, where he used some of the money his father had given him to get a place on a boat to Indonesia. 'How big was the boat?' I asked.

'Small,' he said, 'about from here to here,' pointing at either end of the room. Little more than a rowboat, I thought, how could it possibly cross the ocean? On that boat, you forgot everything, Ahmad tells me. You forgot about life, how you lived, or who you were. Men, women and children are all packed together and people were vomiting from seasickness and fear. It was a sixteen-hour trip, with no food or water, and no knowing what lay ahead.

On arrival in Indonesia, Ahmad and the other refugees were caught by the Indonesian police. Because they were refugees they were not jailed, but regardless they had nowhere to go. Indonesia was like living in limbo, shuffled back and forwards endlessly between hotels by authorities. There was no direction or purpose and no way to create your life anew.

To buy a place on the boat to Australia, people gave away any money they had left, or any last pieces of jewellery, perhaps their wedding rings. Two hundred and thirty people were boarded onto one small boat, and, as on the boat from Kuala Lumpur, this was a boat where you forgot everything. You were nobody again and it was too horrible to think about. You were a piece of forgotten luggage floating along the sea, buffeted by salty waves and storms or burnt by the hot sun; there was no point in calling for help, because there was no one there to rescue you.

The boat was too heavy and rocked from side to side. Everyone was ordered to throw any luggage overboard. Ahmad had been carrying two bags with him, and now his last possessions in the world sunk to the bottom of the sea. The trip was to last for seventeen days. On the fourteenth day the food and water ran out. People were trying to drink seawater, there were babies on board, and people were dying.

The last ten hours, Ahmad told me, were spent preparing for death: 'Only God was there for me now, and, if I was to die, then I would die. I cleaned my heart and mind of everything, there was only one people in the world, and only one god, who is everybody's god, and I gave everything to him. I loved everybody then, inside my heart, even the people who had hung my uncle, even Saddam's men who had taken me and beaten me. There was only one earth, only one humanity, we were all people, God was there, I emptied everything from myself, and my love was for everybody.'

If any part of Ahmad's story touched me most, it was when he told me this. People can die with hearts filled with bitterness, clinging to the poisons of hatred or revenge, and yet Ahmad lay with nothing but the clothes that he wore, having been through what he had been through, and was ready to die with a heart filled with love.

The cold walls of politics

Arriving in Darwin, Ahmad saw people of all different colours and appearances. Maybe I am in heaven, he thought, until someone woke him and told him where he was. Perhaps now a time had finally come to create a place for himself in the world.

But instead he was greeted with detention centres and Woomera, and with pain and sickness from all his injuries which the centres refused to treat properly. His application for asylum was rejected, and why? Because his interpreter spoke Arabic from Syria, which is different from Kurdish Arabic, and which Ahmad can only understand 'ten percent,' as he told me.

You never know what new challenges will be around the next corner, but after surviving all that he had, you would not have thought that Ahmad's next big challenge would have been with the cold walls of bureaucracy and the manipulations of politics.

Eventually, with the right interpreter, Ahmad's appeal was accepted, although even then it was only a visa for temporary protection when stability for once in his life would have been the greatest gift. Finally, the prolonged frustration and isolation of the detention centres was over, and it was out into Australia. Again, as so many times before in his life, Ahmad was alone, with no language or friends. He lived by himself in an apartment in the city centre of Canberra for one month until gradually he began to meet new people. Now he has a house and is working, but his protection is still only temporary.

The earth is my home and humanity is my family

Ahmad told me about his life in Australia, but it is another story in itself, and I will not tell it here. He is not perfect, he told me, but he is still strong as a human being. He will need this strength, because at twenty-one his life has only just begun. On the television, bombs fall, Saddam is toppled and now chaos reigns. If Ahmad's family is alive, then they are there somewhere, amidst the chaos. There are speeches about freedom, liberty and democracy. But these leaders will not bring freedom, Ahmad tells me. They are not sincere in their hearts – they talk of freedom, but freedom is not in words and speeches. 'They do not understand what freedom is, and they do not want it for us.'

When he says 'us', I do not think that he means just Kurdish people, or just Iraqis. 'Us' is humanity, all of humanity together. 'The earth is my country and human beings are my family,' Ahmad tells me. Fighting over different countries, or where people come from, is to act like children, fighting over toys and playthings, stealing one another's dolls. God is there for all of us, and, although there will always be sadness, there is also life, and in life there are many things that we can share with one another to make our time here on this earth, for all of humanity, as beautiful as possible.

Acknowledgements

A Last Resort? The National Inquiry into Children in Immigration Detention (http://www.hreoc.gov.au/human_rights/children_detention_report/summaryguide/index.html) is quoted with permission from HREOC.

David Campbell's 'Men in Green' on pages 74 and 79 is quoted with permission from Judy Campbell.

The quotation on page 115 is from A. Adelson and R. Lapides, *Lodz Ghetto: A Community Under Siege*, Viking Penguin, USA 1989.

Australians Against Racism could not run the competitions or edit these anthologies without the help of a huge number of volunteers, sponsors and supporters. These projects are run entirely by volunteers: we have no paid staff. There is No Place like Home 2004 and Australia is Refugees! 2002 owe everything to the following people and organisations, and to the unnamed parents and teachers who got behind the project.

There is No Place like Home 2004
Yasmin Aleem, Allen&Unwin, Australian Curriculum Studies Association, Australian Education Union, Australian Education Union (SA), Robin Ballantyne, Andrew Bartlett, Deslie Billich,

Tony Birch, *Bonzer!*, Jane Bromley, Geraldine Brooks, Marg Castles, Sheleyah Courtney, Mary Crock, Sonja Dechian, Jenni Devereaux, Burr Dodd, Janet Donald, Rob Durbridge, Sally Edsall, Dan Farmer, Foundation for Young Australians, Ron and Sue Fraser, Angelo Gavrielatos, Zeny Giles, Morris Gleitzman, Kathleen Graham, The Graham Smith Peace Trust Inc, Fiona Hardie and Sandy Grant, Hardie Grant Publishing, Dennis and Rhonda Haskell, Rosanne Hawke, Anita Heiss, Susan Hopgood, Judy Horacek, Lolo Houbein, Lyndall Hough, Independent Education Union, Virginia Jones, Nicholas Jose, George Karoly, John Kaye, V. Kelliher, Jean Kent, Shelley Kulperger, Carmen Lawrence, Tom Mann, Kelly Martin, Sandy McCutcheon, Meme McDonald, Cathy McGuire, Heather Millar, Neil Montieth, Gaylene Morgan, Kerry Nettle, NSW Teachers Federation, Jacqueline Patrick, CJR and LJ Payne, Project Safecom, Boori Pryor, Margaret Reynolds, Suzanne Rutland, SA Writers Centre, Eva Sallis, Roger Sallis, Joanne Scicluna, Simone Senisin, School Libraries Association SA, School of Communication Culture and Languages Victoria University, School of Social Work and Social Policy University of South Australia, Jack Smit, Julie Smith, Sue Smith, Soroptimist International South Perth, Jonathan Stratton, Shaun Tan, Theosophical Order of Service, Ray R Tyndale, United Nations Association Australia, Victoria Chambers, Wakefield Press, Alan Wheatley, World Heart Music Festival, Edie Wright, Arnold Zable.

Australia Is Refugees! 2002

Phillip Adams, A Just Australia/Australians For Just Refugee Programs, Allen & Unwin, Ian Anderson, Australian Education Union, Australian Education Union – South Australia, Australian Refugees Association, BJ and A Baker, Blue Expressions Framing SA, Geraldine Brooks, Brunswick Street Bookshop, Julian Burnside, Errin Davis, Sonja Dechian, James Dent, Jenni Devereaux, Kate Durham, Dan Farmer, Ann Feather, Derek

Fielding, Malcolm Fraser, Ron and Sue Fraser, Mary Freer, Fremantle Refugee Support Project, Raimond Gaita, Helen Garner, Libby Gleeson, Fiona Hardie and Sandy Grant, Hardie Grant Publishers, Virginia Gordon, Lolo Houbein, Independent Education Union Australia, John Kinsella, Katie Langmore, Kevin Liston, Sam Malin, The CUB Malthouse, Kelly Martin, Tom Mann, Meme McDonald, Bern McPhee, Metro/Screen Education, Heather Millar, National Committee on Human Rights Education, NSW Teachers Federation, Oz Positive, CJR and LJ Payne, Margaret Reynolds United Nations Association Australia, Rural Australians for Refugees, Eva Sallis, Roger Sallis, School of Social Work and Social Policy, University of South Australia, Selina, Tom Shapcott, Albert Shelling, Beverley Sherry, Jack Smit, MDH and REJ Smith, South Australians for Justice for Refugees, Jo Stanley, Victoria Chambers, Victorian Trades Hall Council, Nadia Wheatley, Morag White, John Wishart, Ulrike Zimmermann.

About the Writers Now

Nastassia Allen

I am sixteen and live in the Hills area of Sydney with my brother and sister, who are both eleven years old. Currently in Year Eleven, I study English, French, maths, visual arts, biology and chemistry. I am passionate about languages, drama and in particular art, which is why I would like to enter a creative field when I leave school, but I am also very interested in psychology and sciences like genetics. During my spare time, I love to paint and listen to rock music, and I take part in drama productions and play the clarinet in the school band and orchestra.

Christine Chung

I'm currently in my first year studying business and marketing in Melbourne. I'm looking forward to getting my degree in the next couple of years so that I can apply to become a permanent citizen in Australia and put my knowledge and skills to good use out there in the business world. In my spare time I enjoy listening to music, reading a good book and going to the movies. Writing this story is by far one of the best choices I've ever made – and I have many people to thank for that. I'm very grateful that I could speak out about my experiences and actually be heard – not too many people get this opportunity. So, THANK YOU.

Jessie Clifton

Lives in Western Australia.

Nicholas James Cooper

Nicholas is originally from England and currently lives in country NSW. He was educated at St Josephs College, Hunters Hill and has a commerce degree from Sydney University where he was a resident for three years and house treasurer at St John's College. His other main interest is in acting, and he has had several roles, including in the film *Lantana*. His sporting interests are athletics and rock climbing.

Nitya Dambiec

On completing Year Twelve, I had a desire to see the world, and that is what I did. I also wanted to make good use of my time, and so I have ended up in Mongolia working at the Lotus Children's Centre (www.lotuschild.org). I have been spending my time learning to walk on ice when it is minus 35 degrees outside, unsuccessfully trying to keep a warm fire and helping care for 130 babies and children of all ages, as they learn to walk and talk and grow. So far, we've managed to get stuck in the snow in the countryside just in time to watch the sun set over the mountains, had the sewage overflow in our apartment (twice), and had a fire in our house in the middle of the night. I have found a new home here, and it is a wonderful and rewarding place to be.

André Dao

André lives with his family in Melbourne. He is a budding writer, which is to say, he tries to knock out a story every now and again. Writing and learning the story of his aunt as she came to Australia was sobering, thought-provoking and deeply moving. He is currently in Year Twelve and is hoping later to travel the world, including visits to France and Vietnam. His life motto is, 'Weaseling out of things is important to learn. It's what separates us from the animals . . . except the weasel.'

Darko Djukic

Darko was born in 1986 in a Croatian town called Gospic. He lives with his mother and sister and says that he couldn't imagine his life without them. In 2004 he did chemistry, biology, mathematical methods, English as a second language, information processing management, Croatian and Serbian for his Victorian Certificate of Education. He likes to read books and listen to music. He also loves nightclubs and going out with friends. He would like to become a doctor or do anything in the medical field.

Kuach Deng

I live in the city now, in Sydney, with my sister and some more family. I'm going to high school and getting used to being in Australia. It's important for me to go to school and get a good education. I like to play sport, and I really like soccer and basketball. I've made some friends here, and sometimes I meet some of the people from where I lived before, too.

Lual Makuei Deng

Lives in Victoria.

Amelia Easton

I'm in Year Eleven and my favourite subjects at school are legal studies and biology. When I leave school I'd like to study law and economics or commerce. In my spare time I like to read (especially about politics and history), write, hang out with my friends or play netball. I have a part time job at a bakery. The person I'd most like to meet is Gough Whitlam.

Deng Elia

I live in Queensland with some of my brothers and sisters. The most important thing for me right now is to go to school and learn and get more education. I like to play basketball most of all, and when I leave school I'd like to become a professional player and play with one of the good basketball teams. I play and train every weekend.

Caitlin Gardiner

I am the eldest child in a family of four and I am the only girl. I was born in Broome, Western Australia on 8 August 1988 but I have lived in Victoria for most of my life. I turn seventeen in 2005 and I am currently studying literature, psychology, legal studies, maths, Japanese, English and religion in Year Eleven. I recently returned from a three-month home-stay in Japan, which was an enlightening and enjoyable experience, and gave me a good grounding for the study of Japanese, which I have been studying for five years. I enjoy reading a variety of genres and love to watch a decent movie. I hope to travel more in the future but have no clear plans yet apart from completing my Victorian Certificate of Education to the best of my ability.

Sarah Gelbart

I was born in and grew up in Melbourne with my parents and younger sister. My family have always been close, and through-out my childhood I would look forward to Friday night dinners together at my grandparents' home. I wrote this story several years ago about their journey to Australia. The process was difficult, but I learnt a lot about myself along the way. I have now finished school and am studying Medicine at the University of Melbourne. I am also a leader at my Youth Movement, which I thoroughly enjoy. Aside from that, I love sports and learning languages. This project provided me with a great opportunity to better understand my heritage and come to appreciate my home here in Australia. For that I am very grateful.

Irene Guo

Irene is your everyday thirteen-year-old girl who thinks fun is the key to life. She lives by the mottos 'smile and the world will smile with you' and 'live life to the extreme!' She likes to try out new things and to know by the end of the day that she has tried something new. Irene likes to swim, play netball, volleyball, ride her bike, surf the net and play on her PS2. Her favourite season is summer because it means she can go swimming everyday. Irene hasn't even thought about what she will do when she is grown up, but when the time comes she'll know. The only thing she is sure about is that she wants to travel the world and see all the exotic places she has been hearing about.

Salima Haidary

Salima is in Year Eleven in the Australian Capital Territory. She is really looking forward to going to College and says she has already chosen her subjects and met some of her teachers. At school her friends are Hallie, Ramona and Kelly. In her free time she likes to spend time with her family. In the future she hopes to study medicine and would love to go back to Afghanistan to provide antenatal care for mothers and babies. Too many women die because there is no one to care for them.

Felicity Rose Hann

Hello, my name is Felicity Rose Hann (aka Flick) and I am the author of the story about Hal Hart. I have always had a fascination with writing. It has been my saviour. I was born in 1991 and am just one of your average thirteen-year-olds. Along with writing and reading I love the arts such as singing and acting. Last year I participated in a local production called 'No No Nanette'. I have just gone into high school – a very interesting new world. I play netball and enjoy being with my friends – without them my world would crumble. So that is the tiniest amount of happy information from my life. I hope you enjoy my story as I am aiming for many more in the future. Thank you and please enjoy my story.

Jay Higson-Coleing

I was born in Sydney in 1992. I now live on the mid-north coast of New South Wales with my mum and dad and my three-year-old dog called Kimee. I am twelve years old, but I was eleven when I wrote this story. I am now in Year Seven. My favourite subjects at school are design and technology, sport and English, and I don't mind maths and Indonesian. I like going to the movies, tennis, dancing and hanging out with my friends. When I grow up I want to either go to university and study fashion design, or go to NIDA (National Institute of Dramatic Arts) and be an actress.

Carla Johnson

Hi, I'm Carla and I'm seventeen years old. I am the older of two siblings. I am from the little island down south, Tasmania, and I live along the beautiful north-west coast. I have lived here all my life, however after I finish my studies, I am going to university in Hobart to study journalism, photography and media, as I want to become a TV journalist. My other ambitions include travelling, languages, music, singing, dancing, which I have been doing for twelve years, and athletics. In December 2005 I am going to Japan to further my Japanese language skills. I hope my trip to Japan will be the start of much international travel, and that I am able to meet new people and find out their stories, just as I did with my Australians Against Racism story. I wrote this story because of my strong opinions on racism and love for this country and all its citizens.

Atem Jok

I was born overseas and crossed the globe to Australia. I am here for further study, but now I am a high school student. My future plans are to finish university and obtain a PhD in political science. Then I think I will go back to where I was born. I like to support justice and human rights. I feel particularly strongly about the government of my country's treatment of people and asylum seekers, and I am interested in international law.

Hallie Kent

Hallie is sixteen and is in Year Eleven. She likes English, IT and Japanese. In 2004 she travelled to Japan. In her free time she likes to be with her friends, go shopping and see movies, or listening to music, playing volleyball, talking on the phone, going to the pool in summer and ice skating in winter. She also likes the beach and body surfing, and her break dancing and hip hop dance classes. Hallie is involved in an organisation called CREATE. This is an organisation that is all about young people in out-of-home care. She has participated in interstate conferences and acted as an Australian Capital Territory representative for CREATE at these conferences. Hallie wants to make a difference in our community.

Jasmina Kevric

I was born in Bosnia. I arrived in Australia in 1999 and prior to that I lived in Germany for three years. My story 'Long Road to Happiness' is a personal account of my life. Writing stories about my past allows me to express emotions that I otherwise would not be able to. Having witnessed death and experienced pain and struggle, it was tough to return to normal life. However, I learned how to ignore certain things and only concentrate on what I thought was important and follow my dreams and aspirations. I am currently studying medicine at the University of Melbourne, and I hope to travel to under-developed and war-torn countries and use my position to help people and make a difference.

Mert Korkusuz

Mert is a Year Eight student. He lives in Sydney with his mother, father and his younger brother, Evren. Mert enjoys camping, travelling, family outings, socialising with his friends, reading, writing, listening to music and playing the piano. Chess games and computer games are other activities that he does for enjoyment. Last but not least on the list is a variety of sports including tennis, swimming, soccer, and basketball. Basketball has a very special place in Mert's life. He enjoys the game so much that he dreams about becoming a basketball player when he grows up (as well as being a geneticist or having a career in robotics). Mert is concerned about the mountain-tall problems of the world we are living in today, particularly the conflicts between the nations, wars, and all sorts of discrimination including racism. 'If one of these days I am confronted with a genie granting me with three wishes, my wishes would be peace, health and equal opportunities for everybody in the world, particularly the children,' Mert says.

David Maney

David lives and works in Adelaide. He is currently completing a Bachelor of Creative Arts – Creative Writing. He is a regular contributor to the university newspaper as well as the sub-editor of the lifestyle section and editor of the literary pages. In the spare hours of night he maintains a blog (www.boytoworld.blogspot.com) which he shamelessly promotes wherever possible. David hopes to be an influential literary figure in the future, but as yet hasn't worked out how he will achieve this goal.

Hope Mathumbu

I migrated to Australia from South Africa two years ago with my mother and younger sister because my mother managed to get a job nursing. I am currently studying Year Twelve and hope to get into university to study journalism so I can be a foreign correspondent and bring some truth to the news! I love reading and writing, and all forms of knowledge. It's a really great thing to step out of your circle, or to completely not have one at all, in order to understand people – there is that added freedom of objectivity – because you are the lone drifter and in some ways a catalyst for change. Writing the story meant a lot to me, because having someone trust you that much for no apparent reason except to help you win a competition is completely surreal. In retrospect, the story made me think how frivolously erroneous the notions and interpretations of 'patriotism' and 'home' really are. Over-exercising these terms is a huge problem in our current society – they lead to prejudice, bureaucracies, fights for dominance and wars. These are very scary times we are living in, and it's scary to witness what people must do for just a single taste of a different world – why can't we just welcome them?

Kiah McIntyre-Cooper

I am thirteen years old and live in Melbourne, Victoria. I have seventeen pets including ten fish, four frogs, two dogs (Jake and Sam) and one horse named Cruise. My hobby is horse riding, I do it every single weekend. I am in Year Nine and I am enjoying it.

Luke D Ryan

I am twelve years old. At the end of 2004, I received a Community Involvement Award from the Australian House of Representatives for my 'personal pursuit of excellence' after being nominated by my school. I love to read and play scrabble with my family and in the summertime go to the beach. I study the piano and play the clarinet in the school band and have studied dance. I play sports: cricket, hockey and rugby league. I enjoy writing especially about things that matter to me. I have always been interested in current affairs. I consider myself fortunate to have received a good education. I hope to study journalism and law and, of course, be a writer when I am older.

Sam

Lives in New South Wales.

Victoria Shaw

Victoria comes from Western Australia. She has a very annoying eight-year-old brother who often bosses her around and she absolutely hates it. Her favourite hobbies include tennis, cricket, chess, table tennis and swimming. She dislikes gymnastics and discus. Her favourite subjects include maths, geography and woodwork. Victoria loves to be around her friends and her favourite pastime is reading. Victoria's favourite author is Brian Jacques, the author of the Redwall Abbey series and her favourite book is *Rakkety Tam*. She loves music and plays the clarinet.

She is also in the school band. Her dream is to become a politician or a lawyer when she grows up.

Kyle Sellick Smith

I grew up on the mid-north coast of New South Wales, and completed my schooling and Higher School Certificate in 2004. I am currently on leave from university where I plan to study the Bachelor of Business in Convention and Event Tourism Management, commencing 2006. This year I have been working as a labourer in various trades, ranging from roof tiling to plumbing and painting. I have successfully gained employment at Falls Creek, Victoria, for the snow season this year, which I'm looking forward to very much. My interests include surfing, snowboarding, guitar, fishing, golf, rugby league and union, and soccer. I'm sick of the white man putting the black man down with his money, power and cultural dominance. I want the black man to rise up, show determination and show the white man that he is strong. Just because the wealth of the world isn't equally divided doesn't mean that the white man can always keep more than his fair share. Peace to the world and I hope that black power lives on!

Lazar Stamenkovic

Lives in South Australia.

Ramona Strang

Ramona is in Year Eleven in the Australian Capital Territory. Ramona would like to be a dentist, forensic scientist, teacher or a lawyer. Ramona's hobbies are typing, chatting to her friends, writing letters and emails, socialising, indoor soccer, going overseas, going to theme parks, singing, helping others, babysitting, surfing the internet, shopping, listening to music, talking on the mobile phone. She has a number of achievements, including awards from 40 hour Famine; United Nations High Commission for Refugees; Red Shield Appeal; and Australians Against Racism. Her friends mean a great deal to her. Her friends have had a strong influence on her; they have supported her through the good times and the bad. They always see the good things in life and try to block out the bad.

Edith Tom

I'm a sixteen-year-old studying Year Ten. I belong in a family of five and I have a younger brother who is twelve this year, and the fifth member of our family is the most beautiful Maltese terrier in the world, Aiko. We live in south-western Sydney. I was born in Australia and my parents have been here for about twenty years. My hobbies and interests include dramatic performance, debating, humanitarian issues, horror movies, reading, playing netball and basketball, music and the occult. I am a strong believer in the power of compassion, and I think the future can be filled with hope. I guess my only dislikes are people who look down on others, whether it be because of race, religion or appearance. I also believe that although we have the right to bind people from doing harm to others, no one has the right to take away the chance of life from another human being. I always feel blessed because of the opportunities that I have been given, and I think that the world can be a wondrous place if only we try to make it that way. My greatest hope would be that I could share some of the blessings that I have experienced with the rest of the world. Finally, I would like to say that, contrary to what you may be thinking, I am not an idealist.

Fabienne Trevere

Fabienne attends high school in Sydney, where she has been involved in promoting human rights and social justice issues. She coordinates her school's Amnesty International group and initiated a program to sponsor a sister school in Afghanistan, through the charity Mahboba's Promise. Fabienne is also very interested in international relations, and this year will be attending the national United Nations Youth Conference as a delegate for New South Wales. Fabienne is an ambassador for ChilOut, the organisation through which she met Nahid, the subject of her story. ChilOut campaigns for the release of all children from immigration detention.

Henry Upton

I am fifteen years old and am currently studying Year Ten in Adelaide. My passions lie in the fields of English and academics. I also love music and computer games. I first heard my grandfather's story as a child and feel now that I am older, it is an experience worth sharing. (Henry is the winner of the *Advertiser* Young Writer of the Year Award 2005 – eds)

Fernanda Valdés Chepe

I was born in Santiago, Chile, in 1984 and came to Australia in 1986. I was raised in Sydney's south-western suburbs of Cabramatta and Fairfield, where I gained insight into the beauty and the difficulties faced by immigrants. I am currently studying high school teaching, and I hope to become a dedicated teacher. I also aspire to contribute to the fields of educational policy or critical theory, but I hope to always continue writing.

Najeeba Wazefadost

Najeeba came to Australia in September 2000 before the Olympic Games. She is a refugee from Bamyan, Afghanistan. She is a ChilOut (Children Out of Detention) ambassador. Najeeba would love to be a politician. Her dream is to show Australia that she will be a person who will do her best for her country. One of her other dreams is to see her relatives again.

Yusra

Lives in Victoria.

Iman Zayegh

I am currently in Year Ten in Victoria. I wrote this story in the hope of being able to let readers know part of what happened in many of the war-torn countries in the past. I wish to give people a broader understanding of the living conditions that many people experienced during the wars that took place, and how they suffered and endured many hardships to reach where they are now. In my spare time I love to read books, particularly teenage fiction, and take the time to curl up with a nice story whenever I get the chance. My aim is to do well in the Victorian Certificate of Education and study medicine to become a paediatrician and help sick children recover from their illnesses.

Also from Wakefield Press

Dark Dreams

Australian refugee stories by young writers aged 11–20 years

Edited by Sonja Dechian, Heather Millar and Eva Sallis

Dark Dreams is an anthology of essays, interviews and short stories written by children and young adults aged 11–20 years. These young writers relate or imaginatively recreate the story of someone who came to Australia as a refugee.

This is a unique book in Australia. The stories are the finest of hundreds collected through an unprecedented nationwide schools competition, devised by writer Eva Sallis and run by Australians Against Racism Inc.

The essays and stories represent many different countries. Some focus on survival, some on horrors, some on the experiences and alienation of a new world. Some are stories of refugees still living in detention centres in Australia.

These stories are shocking, moving, and at times funny. Some are written with the quirky humour of children, others show the frank compassion and honest surprise of young Australians as they encounter experiences more terrible than their own. Some are gut-churning stories from young children just starting to rebuild lives here.

Across the collection, there emerges the recurrent theme of friendship: friendships lost, broken, remembered and found, now in Australia.

For more information visit www.wakefieldpress.com.au

Praise for Dark Dreams

'The stories are wide-ranging and powerful. But at the centre is the simple truth that refugees are courageous people and the political structures that deny them basic human rights are abhorrent. Every Australian should read this book. It is a vital contribution to our country's complex moral history.'

– Bruce Elder, *Sydney Morning Herald*

'These salutary tales, told by young refugees or by older refugees to young people, have a purity and an appealing lack of artifice . . . What is most moving is the unadulterated admiration and lack of scepticism that emerges, so rare in mainstream media portrayals of immigrants.'

– Anne Susskind, *Bulletin*

'. . . this moving, illuminating, extraordinary collection is filled with the faces we have been denied.'   – Katharine England, *Advertiser*

'I read the essays with curiosity and a great deal of emotion. They would melt the hardest heart. The real treasures are the stories told by young refugees themselves, and by the children of people who fled to Australia a generation ago. Some of the more recent arrivals here have struggled with a language not their own, and have produced stories we will never be able to forget.'   – Helen Garner

'We have not been allowed to know the (recent) refugees as human beings – as men, women and children, as mothers and husbands, sons and daughters. These stories change all that and force a personal response from the reader. What a pity Australia's bigots can't be persuaded to read these accounts. It might, just might, make them more understanding and compassionate.'   – Phillip Adams

Wakefield Press is an independent publishing and
distribution company based in Adelaide, South Australia.
We love good stories and publish beautiful books.
To see our full range of books, please visit our website at
www.wakefieldpress.com.au
where all titles are available for purchase.
To keep up with our latest releases, news and events,
subscribe to our newsletter.

Find us!

Facebook: www.facebook.com/wakefield.press
Twitter: www.twitter.com/wakefieldpress
Instagram: www.instagram.com/wakefieldpress

www.ingramcontent.com/pod-product-compliance
Ingram Content Group Australia Pty Ltd
76 Discovery Rd, Dandenong South VIC 3175, AU
AUHW021244060225
406607AU00001B/2